Impacting Teaching and Learning

Impacting Teaching and Learning

Contemplative Practices, Pedagogy, and Research in Education

Elizabeth Hope Dorman,
Kathryn Byrnes,
and
Jane E. Dalton

ROWMAN & LITTLEFIELD
Lanham • Boulder • New York • London

Published by Rowman & Littlefield
A wholly owned subsidiary of The Rowman & Littlefield Publishing Group, Inc.
4501 Forbes Boulevard, Suite 200, Lanham, Maryland 20706
www.rowman.com

Unit A, Whitacre Mews, 26-34 Stannary Street, London SE11 4AB

British Library Cataloguing in Publication Information Available

Library of Congress Cataloging-in-Publication Data Available

ISBN: 978-1-4758-3634-9 (cloth : alk. paper)
ISBN: 978-1-4758-3635-6 (pbk. : alk. paper)
ISBN: 978-1-4758-3636-3 (electronic)

∞ ™ The paper used in this publication meets the minimum requirements of American National Standard for Information Sciences—Permanence of Paper for Printed Library Materials, ANSI/NISO Z39.48-1992.

Printed in the United States of America

Contents

Foreword

Laura I. Rendón

It never fails. When I address educators and ask them to identify the one or two key competencies that are absolutely essential for students to learn when they graduate from college, we generate two lists, depicting both intellectual and inner aptitudes. The longest competency list that emerges relates to inner-life skills; for example, being authentic, having integrity, working well with others, having a sense of meaning and purpose, seeing the glass half full, practicing presence, developing wisdom, having self-awareness, practicing empathy, seeking justice, and being open to new ideas.

And when I follow up and ask them how much time they spend developing exactly what they consider to be the most important competencies students should have learned when they leave college, there is an awkward silence and sometimes nervous laughter as educators realize that most of what they have done is to focus on traditional measures of learning related to cognitive development.

This simple exercise exemplifies that we are out of balance in education, and it is time to address this imbalance with a newly-fashioned paradigm that appreciates and fosters not only intellectual development, but also abilities that allow an individual to access inner knowing related to emotions, intuition, and wisdom.

Not only are we out of balance, but this is a challenging, complex time when the demands of the teaching profession have become quite overwhelming, necessitating a new perspective that focuses on what and how to teach, as well as on the teacher whose role it is to construct and facilitate a pedagogy of wholeness. There is little professional development training for teachers to work with a pedagogy of wholeness which includes contemplative practices.

To that end, Elizabeth Hope Dorman, Kathryn Byrnes, and Jane E. Dalton have edited a collective trio of books providing invigorating, innovative ways that contemplative pedagogy can deepen the work of teaching and learning in today's P–12 classrooms. What the authors theorize is that contemplative pedagogy that focuses on deep learning experiences and reflective practices can strengthen teaching and learning, while supporting and enhancing teacher development. As suggested by Hawkins (2007), each of the three books complement each other and are arranged to cover three important aspects of meaningful learning experiences.

The first book, *Cultivating a Culture of Learning: Contemplative Practices, Pedagogy, and Research in Education*, attends to the *content of teaching*, with examples of how to integrate contemplative practices in teacher education courses and programs.

The second book, *Impacting Teaching and Learning: Contemplative Practices, Pedagogy, and Research in Education*, addresses the *who that is being taught*, and features current research on the impacts of contemplative practices and pedagogy in teacher education.

The third book, *The Teaching Self: Contemplative Practices, Pedagogy, and Research in Education*, focuses on *who is doing the teaching*, with a focus on the teaching self.

Collectively, these three books are representative of what I call sentipensante (sensing/thinking) pedagogy (Rendón, 2009; Rendón, 2011). A sensing/thinking pedagogy is one that disrupts the entrenched notion that education should focus mainly, if not solely, on developing intellectual abilities such as critical thinking and problem solving. As in sentipensante pedagogy, a more spacious view of education is offered in these three books, one that connects and places into balance outer knowing (intellectual reasoning, rationality, and objectivity) with inner knowing (deep wisdom, sense of wonder, introspection, and emotion).

The books stress the development of the whole person, and that educators should attend to all facets of our humanity—intellectual, social, emotional, and spiritual. In these books is the most cutting-edge information about contemplative pedagogy and its relationship to teacher education, including its uses, its challenges, and its promise. Epistemologically, these books move away from over-privileging Rene Descartes's "I think therefore I am," and toward modeling Audre Lorde's "I feel, therefore I can be free" (1984, p. 100). The authors get it right. Quite simply, education is not just about the mind; it is also about our emotions and about our social and spiritual development.

Book II includes scholarly investigations and research-based practices conducted in diverse educational settings. Important themes from these inquiries emerge which are central to the development and enhancement of teacher education programs. The first theme, highlighted to varying degrees in all chapters, refers to the problems and relevant research questions these studies seek to address. Among these problematic situations is the high-pressure, complex environment in which preservice teachers often find themselves. Stringent demands can create stress, anxiety, and burnout, that can result in educators leaving the teaching profession altogether.

There is also the notion, that in far too many cases, schools still privilege standardized testing and focus on replicable, scripted teacher behaviors. Often lost is attention given to social and emotional learning and the intentness that should be given to holistic student development.

Important research questions are: What is the role of contemplative education in deepening and supporting the exploration of social justice issues? How can faculty deal with resistance to contemplative pedagogies and a social justice curriculum, especially when preservice teachers are white, come from privileged backgrounds, and have little to no preparation to work with students and communities of color?

A teacher education curriculum that includes mindfulness and other contemplative practices and that infuses challenging questions of race, equity, oppression, and privilege, especially in today's charged sociopolitical context, has to be very carefully designed to consider structural impediments, purpose, methods, and sociopolitical context. These points are addressed in one chapter, and a second chapter recognizes forms of resistance to contemplative pedagogy (i.e., religious upbringing, dealing with anxiety triggers).

A second theme is that new research, theories, frameworks, and perspectives need to be developed to guide the evolution of teacher education. These theories and frameworks need to be researched, tested, and disseminated. To capture the impact of contemplative practices on learners is not an easy task. Yet faculty and students in teacher education programs seek and need research evidence that pedagogic practices actually work and under what circumstances they succeed or not.

Also needed is research to document the impact of these practices on teacher candidates both at the preservice level and when they assume full-time teaching responsibilities. Fortunately, readers of this volume are offered diverse methodological approaches and contemplative practices that lift the knowledge base of contemplative education.

Collectively, the research demonstrates that contemplative pedagogy (i.e., mindfulness, labyrinth, visualization, loving-kindness meditation, narrative pedagogy, silent journaling, relational mindfulness, contemplative reading activities, Five Dimensions of Engaged Teaching, and collaborative inquiry, among others) can yield important student outcomes. These outcomes address some of the challenges outlined earlier.

A third theme from the authors' research points to the notion that a new vision of teacher preparation is warranted to include a level of transformation that goes beyond a focus on methods, tips, and techniques. This vision can be guided by the following principles:

- A focus on teachers as human beings, not as machines.
- Support for overall teacher well-being, which includes leading balanced, healthy, satisfying lives.
- A need for teachers to attend to the inner core of their lives, and be in touch with their authentic self, as well as their strengths.
- A need to go beyond focusing on standardized testing and narrow views of student achievement. Instead, there is a compelling need to focus on teaching and cultivating the development of the whole child.
- The realization that teaching requires deep engagement with self and others.
- A focus on relational competence and the importance of developing teacher/student relationships, communicating with empathy, and having awareness of embodied physical and emotional sensations especially during charged moments.

This collection of books plays an integral part in moving education to a new consciousness, one that challenges, if not shatters, hegemonic assumptions about teaching and learning, including the privileging of positivist assumptions about detachment and objectivity, Eurocentrism as the only credible way of knowing, the separation of teacher and student, and the separation of reason from emotion.

What is being offered in these books is a politic of affinity and connectedness, and the ontological view that humanity at its core seeks relationships and a sense of belonging. Thinking and feeling share equal status and become, as Lorde expresses, "a choice of ways and explorations" (1984, p. 101) to seek knowledge and to form truths.

These three books should be required reading, especially for the new generation of students seeking to enter the teaching profession and who believe that values and ethical practices such as community, personal and social responsibility, integrity, truth-telling, and self-reflection must share an equal space with cognitive development in a school classroom. Of significant import is that these books represent a marvelous pedagogic gift from courageous educators who have dared to take risks, have followed their intuition about what an authentic classroom should be, and have stayed true to the original impulse that drove them into the teaching profession.

I imagine that if you have picked up any one of these three books that something inside of you is seeking something different, something authentic, something that speaks to the whole of your being. Look no more. In your hands are exemplars of authentic teacher education, holistic student development, and the cultivation of classrooms guided by rigorous intellectual pursuits and the foundation for building an educational system that aspires to democratic ideals, humanitarianism, culturally responsive practices, and the common good.

In your hands is the foundation for the evolution of a new story of what it means to prepare educators to facilitate student learning in a world that is desperately calling for ethical leaders who can (with intelligence, insight, and wisdom) deal with the contradictions, uncertainties, messiness, and complications of our lives. I applaud this inspiring, ground-breaking work, and encourage you to become an integral part of shaping the new story of education based on wholeness and guided by the ultimate expression of our values—love.

—Laura I. Rendón, author of *Sentipensante (Sensing/Thinking) Pedagogy: Educating for Wholeness, Social Justice and Liberation* (2009)

REFERENCES

Hawkins, D. (2007). *The informed vision: Essays on learning and human nature.* Algora Publishing.

Lorde, A. (1984). *Sister outsider: Essays and speeches.* Berkeley, CA: Crossing Press.

Rendón, L. I. (2009). *Sentipensante (sensing/thinking) pedagogy: Educating for wholeness, social justice and liberation.* Sterling, VA: Stylus Press.

Rendón, L. I. (2011). Cultivating una persona educada: A sentipensante (sensing/thinking) vision of education. *Journal of College and Character, 12*(2), 1–9.

Acknowledgments

This book has been inspired and nurtured by many educators, artists, scholars, and contemplatives. Our heartfelt gratitude to those educators, past and present, who have been instrumental in opening the contemplative path, and to the students whose search for meaning and purpose provided inspiration for and feedback during the journey.

We are grateful to all of those with whom we have had the pleasure of working during the development and publication of this book series. Without the vision and dedication of the volume two contributors—Kira J. Baker-Doyle, Gayle L. Butaud, Jennifer Cannon, Lisa Flook, M. Elizabeth Graue, William L. Greene, Matthew J. Hirshberg, Younghee M. Kim, Per F. Laursen, Roshmi Mishra, Evan E. Moss, Shelley Murphy, Anne Maj Nielsen, Elsie L. Olan, and Vanessa M. Villate—this series would not be possible. Thank you. Each unique voice and perspective offers a richly complex tapestry of ways to integrate contemplative practice, pedagogy, and research into the field of teacher education. We extend a special thanks to Tom Koerner, Carlie Wall, and Emily Tuttle at Rowman & Littlefield for their support during this process. We are also especially grateful to Laura I. Rendón, Professor Emerita at the University of Texas–San Antonio, and author of *Sentipensante (Sensing/Thinking) Pedagogy: Educating for Wholeness, Social Justice, and Liberation* for writing the profound, inspired forewords for each of the three volumes in this series.

We feel especially humbled by the collaboration, support, friendship, and collegiality that has developed over the years as we, the editors, worked together to develop, refine, and publish this book series. We are honored to curate such a meaningful, inspired and inspiring series of books for future generations of teacher educators, educators, and students.

Introduction

Elizabeth Hope Dorman, Fort Lewis College,
Durango, Colorado;
Kathryn Byrnes, Bowdoin College,
Brunswick, Maine;
Jane E. Dalton, University of North Carolina
at Charlotte, Charlotte, North Carolina

Cultivating a culture of learning in education demands courageous commitment and willingness to step into the unknown and model authentic engagement through compassionate, experiential, personal practice. Contemplative pedagogy cultivates self-awareness, intrapersonal and interpersonal skills, and deepens learning through practices such as breath awareness, meditation, silence, Lectio Divina, and the arts. As with all emergent curriculum, timely discourse is needed to illuminate the multiple ways in which contemplative pedagogy strengthens teaching and learning in classrooms and supports teacher development.

Typically, teacher education dedicates significant time to build capacities learned from external authorities with an overemphasis on tips, tricks, and techniques of the profession. Rubrics, assessments, instructional strategies, curriculum mapping, and classroom management all privilege rational and empirical knowing across disciplines. Yet, if educators are prepared to rely solely on external authorities as a gauge for pedagogical decisions, then they fail to develop their full capacities, limiting their effectiveness.

Teaching and learning at its best is one of the most elemental of human exchanges and requires that we take responsibility for what, how, and why we teach, and who we are as teachers. Hawkins (2007) suggests that meaningful learning experiences rely on three interdependent facets: "It"—the content of teaching; "Thou"—who is being taught; and "I"—who is teaching.

1

Opening the door to contemplation in teacher education facilitates teacher reflection that deepens content knowledge, relationships with students, and self-awareness of the "I" as teacher.

Teaching demands that we engage all dimensions of human awareness and action. As critical practitioners of the human experience, educators navigate several worlds—the inner realm of one's personal life and the outer worlds of one's classroom, students, and school. As Palmer (1997) observes, "External tools of power have occasional utility in teaching, but they are no substitute for the authority that comes from the teacher's inner life. The clue is in the word itself, which has 'author' at its core" (p. 19).

Educators become the authors of their lives and access the inner life through first-person contemplative experience, second-person dialogue and reflection in community, and third-person narratives of inspiration and guidance, through the integration of contemplative theory, research, and practice in teacher education. The overwhelmingly positive response to our call for chapter submissions demonstrated an interest in the ways in which contemplative theory, research, and practices are being integrated into teacher education globally.

We have organized this scholarship within the field of contemplative teacher education into three books that address the following themes: *Cultivating a Culture of Learning, Impacting Teaching and Learning,* and *The Teaching Self.* Together, these books offer varying insights into the multiple ways that contemplative theory, practices, and research appear in teacher education. In each book, critical, global perspectives address the challenges of implementation along with the benefits of contemplative practices and pedagogy.

The first book focuses on the "It," the integration of contemplative practices in teacher education courses and programs, which is often the most salient and pragmatic approach for teacher educators. The second book addresses the "Thou," current research on the impacts of contemplative practices and pedagogy in teacher education. The third book returns our attention to the teaching self, the "Who." It is our hope that these three volumes will contribute to the ongoing dialogue about contemplative pedagogy in teacher education.

The second book in this series, *Impacting Teaching and Learning: Contemplative Practices, Pedagogy, and Research in Education,* demonstrates research-based practices from a variety of teacher education programs, bringing together a rich collection of voices from diverse settings. The contributors share their diverse methodological research investigating the varied ways learners respond to contemplative practices and pedagogies, and the skills and dispositions that contemplative approaches cultivate in preservice teachers. This volume captures ways in which contemplative pedagogy can influence student outcomes and raises the knowledge base of contemplative education. Authors explore challenges faced institutionally, with students, and personally. The following paragraphs offer highlights from the nine chapters in this book.

Chapter 1, "Encounters with the Soul in Teacher Preparation," by William L. Greene and Younghee M. Kim, shares voices that serve as reminders that, while teachers may feel like they are swimming against a current of status quo pedagogy, there are important reasons for balancing information and critical thinking with deeper and transformative encounters. Preparing for the responsibility of transformative teaching means preparing oneself to enter the sacred space of the classroom and to lead with head, heart, and soul. Ultimately, transformative teaching and learning is, at its essence, an act of the spirit.

Chapter 2, "Cultivating Mindful Teachers: Using a Mindfulness-Based Teaching Approach with Student Teachers," by Vanessa M. Villate and Gayle L. Butaud, discusses the stressors that student teachers experience as they navigate between the demands of their teaching assignment and the requirements of the university supervisors. The authors utilize a reflective tool, a Mindfulness-Based Teaching Approach, developed by Lauren Alderfer, six times in a semester to introduce student teachers to a mindfulness perspective. Student teachers were able to be more calm and focused with their teaching responsibilities and with their students.

Chapter 3, "Cultivating Reflective Teaching Practice through Mindfulness," by Evan E. Moss, Matthew J. Hirshberg, Lisa Flook, and M. Elizabeth Graue, discusses reflective practice to encompass "mindful reflection," which they propose as a mode of reflection that will have the greatest impact on preservice and professional teachers. Mindful reflection is present-moment-centered awareness characterized by openness and equanimity, allowing teachers to better understand and regulate their assumptions, motivations, affect, and cognitions, supporting teacher well-being and student achievement.

Chapter 4, "Preparing Teachers for the Classroom: Mindfulness Awareness Practice in Preservice Education Curriculum," by Shelley Murphy, reports on a study that investigated former preservice teachers' experiences of being introduced to mindfulness practices within their preservice education program. It outlines their attitudes and perceptions toward learning about mindfulness within the core curriculum of their program and the impact of these practices while they were students and as graduates teaching in their own classrooms.

Chapter 5, "Contemplative Teacher Education, Teacher Identity, and Relationship-Building Strategies," by Anne Maj Nielsen and Per F. Laursen, describes a project at a university college in Denmark in which two classes within the teacher education program were adapted to include contemplative teaching in relational competence. The study suggests that the preservice teachers' personal experiences and mindful awareness training, together with their commitment to using their knowledge and experiences of relationship building, stand out as important resources for their future education and teaching careers.

Chapter 6, "Narrative Pedagogy as a Mindful Contemplative Practice: Discovering Preservice Teachers' Mindful Presence," by Elsie L. Olan and Roshmi Mishra, demonstrates how the use of narrative pedagogy as a mindful contemplative practice encourages preservice teachers to discover their mindful presence by experiencing introspective reflection, awareness, and Karelaia's (2014) four stages of mindful decision making. This chapter demonstrates how narrative pedagogy as a mindful contemplative practice offers a new and emerging approach for preservice teachers to discover their mindful presence and decision making.

Chapter 7, "Mindfulness, Student Resistance, and the Limits of Fast-Track Teacher Prep," by Jennifer Cannon, examines the challenges and possibilities of utilizing mindfulness in the context of an urban, fast-track teacher preparation program that introduces preservice secondary teachers to antiracism pedagogy and provides a sociopolitical framework for understanding systems of oppression. Utilizing student voices, this chapter begins to make meaning of student resistance to mindfulness practice, paying careful attention to how structural aspects of the teacher preparation program influence these outcomes.

Chapter 8, "Nurturing the Inner Core through the Five Dimensions of Engaged Teaching," by Elizabeth Hope Dorman, investigates how Weaver and Wilding's engaged teaching framework (2013) was implemented to cultivate the inner dimensions of preservice teachers' experience within the context of contemporary schooling. The contemplative approach described in this chapter has implications for supporting preservice teachers' sustainability as educators and human beings.

Chapter 9, "'There Was This Moment When I Realized': A Framework for Examining Mindful Moments in Teaching," by Kira J. Baker-Doyle, examines the "mindful moments" of teachers, times when teachers experience a shift in awareness about their work. It provides a framework which can support teachers and teacher educators in identifying moments of mindfulness. In addition, contexts that nurture positive emotions are described based on the results of a study of the emotional ecologies of teachers' mindful moments. When teachers collaborate or have the opportunity to engage in creative expression, mindful moments are more likely to foster hope, happiness, and a sense of possibility.

REFERENCES

Hawkins, D. (2007). *The informed vision: Essays on learning and human nature.* New York: Algora Publishing.

Palmer, P. J. (1997). The heart of a teacher: Identity and integrity in teaching. *Change Magazine, 29*(6), 14–21.

Chapter One

Encounters with the Soul in Teacher Preparation

William L. Greene and Younghee M. Kim,
Southern Oregon University, Ashland, Oregon

Creating the conditions for transformative learning and soulful connections in public education requires courage, vision, and a commitment to fostering development of the whole person (Miller, 2006; 2010). To be prepared to do this, teacher candidates need opportunities to experience learning that supports exploration of their innermost sense of self and that honors their natural desire to find meaning in their life's work. Tending to the inner life of teachers can strengthen their commitment to and passion for teaching because it reconnects them with their core qualities (Korthagen, Kim, & Greene, 2013) and their authenticity as individuals (Palmer, 1998).

We became concerned that our pedagogy, too often, fell short in providing conditions and opportunities for our students to connect with their own wholeness as human beings in ways that would sustain them through their early years of teaching. Our emphasis on developing *the inner person* is similar to Miller's (2010) description of transformative teaching. In contrast to more common approaches in public education that focus on the transmission of information and transaction of thinking processes between people, transformative teaching seeks to integrate "wisdom, compassion, and sense of purpose in one's life" to whatever subject or curriculum is being taught (Miller, 2010, p. 30).

For us, this does not mean replacing theory or discipline-based content with self-development but rather recognizing that opportunities to encounter one's own essential nature, or soul as we may think of it in this chapter, should be part of a complete teacher education curriculum. The importance of starting with the soul and teaching from within have been discussed by multiple scholars (e.g., Intrator & Kunzman, 2006; Korthagen, Kim, & Greene, 2013; Miller, 2006; Palmer, 1998). The frameworks presented in this scholarship support the guiding premise here that the most important purpose of our work with new teachers is to remind them who they are, to empower them with a realization of their core strengths, and to give them the experience of reconnecting with those strengths.

We collaborated to reinvent our pedagogy and to orient our curriculum to *start from within*. However, we realized in our earliest years of highlighting the inner person that we were unearthing something *taboo* in the culture of the classroom, much like Ayers and Ayers (2011) described it:

> Teaching the taboo is . . . teaching the suppressed, the banned and the exiled. It's opening our eyes to the lively, dynamic moment before us. It's searching actively for something more. We are in pursuit of fulfillment, reaching for the rest of our humanity. (p. xii)

In spite of that early sense of breaching a traditional classroom norm, we continued for ten years to explore what it meant to bring self-development to the forefront of teacher preparation. We paid close attention to how the more contemplative nature of our pedagogy affected students during their teaching program.

In addition to courses such as Holistic Education, Introduction to Core Reflection, and Social Emotional Learning, we have also introduced transformative approaches in more traditionally content-driven courses, such as Diversity, Educational Psychology, and Philosophic Foundations of Education. Explicit examples featured in these approaches have included regular use of silence and guided visualization to begin class, starting classes with core reflection exercises to promote awareness of being and presence (Korthagen, Kim, & Greene, 2013), identifying living questions as a way to encourage students to hold a space for ambiguity, participating in a circle of trust (Palmer, 2004), building and walking a labyrinth, and creating and enacting a personal rite of passage.

This chapter illustrates how undergraduate and graduate teacher education students responded when the *taboo* (Ayers & Ayers, 2011) dimensions of soul were encountered in the classroom through three activities: core reflection, the class labyrinth, and the personal rite of passage. All three examples consistently produced compelling evidence of transformative learning in class discussions and written comments collected from nine undergraduate and graduate courses over three years at a comprehensive public university in Oregon.

Evidence sources for this chapter included multiple forms of student feedback in weekly online discussion forums, anonymous assignment reflections, course evaluations, and instructors' journal notes. Several program exit interviews were also conducted and video-recorded in which we asked students to comment on the value of their experiences in the three contemplative learning activities summarized below.

ENCOUNTERS WITH SOUL IN THREE ACTIVITIES: CORE REFLECTION, LABYRINTH, AND PERSONAL RITE OF PASSAGE

Student comments provided a wide spectrum of reactions to these class activities from the resistant and skeptical, to the guardedly open, to claims by others that they had experienced a sense of reconnection to who they are and a transformed understanding of the teacher they hoped to become.

Students frequently described their process of self-discovery in terms of expanded presence, even though many also acknowledged their initial hesitation to engage in experiences that seemed out of place in teacher preparation. We have come to expect comments like the following in courses that incorporate contemplative strategies:

> When we first started this class it was difficult for me because it was so different, but I feel like I have grown a lot. I think I learned a lot about myself and how I want to teach. I feel like I have become more spiritually aware. . . . I feel like I am just a lot more conscious about the way I teach and interact with my students. (HD, secondary language arts student teacher, December 2014)

This comment represents a pattern we found common across our classes: students experience something very unexpected in the first class meeting, but as the relationships deepen and the community opens up emotionally, a stronger connection between self and self-as-teacher unfolds, as HD indicated.

Another example in this pattern is the transformational nature of a student's encounter with her soul (or *true self*). It came from a middle-aged early childhood graduate student in a class on holistic education:

> What I have realized in the past few weeks is [that] my reactions to my life's experiences have become disconnected from my true self. Somehow, I have forgotten that I can be vulnerable. I do have fears and needs and yearnings. I don't have to be in control. I don't have to be so strong that I cannot also be soft. I am loving and compassionate. (MH, June 2012)

This quote illustrates that gradually evoking vulnerability through the course allowed her to connect back to qualities she recognized as her true self. Her insight and subsequent behavior in class suggested that her personal revelation reconnected her to her wholeness as a human being. The transformative dimension of self-development is further illustrated in comments from each of the three activities highlighted below.

Core Reflection

We regularly use a practice called core reflection to introduce the concept of presence and to promote deep contact with self and others (Korthagen, Kim, & Greene, 2013). We often begin the first day of a new class with an exercise that invites a sustained connection with a partner in the class. Students are told in advance to expect an unusual form of communication. Each partner gets a timed turn to respond to a question designed to elicit something of the speaker's true nature, their core strengths or qualities. Each partner also takes a turn listening without speaking or responding. Later, the partners share observations of core qualities observed in each other.

In debriefings following this activity, it is not unusual to hear several students say that even though they had known their partner for a long time, they felt more connected to them in those few minutes than they had for months or years. This approach has often set the stage for other types of transformative learning as the class continues.

The idea behind core reflection is that a teacher's awareness of her core qualities—including those that animate her identity and her ideals—determines to a great degree how she will answer the questions, "Who am I and how do I reflect who I am?" (Korthagen & Verkuyl, 2002, p. 44). This becomes a critical point of intersection in the process of exploring one's inner landscape as a teacher: the point where one's identity as a human being intersects with one's professional development (e.g., Palmer, 1998; Korthagen & Verkuyl, 2002).

This is important for new teachers because as they practice recognizing and naming their own core strengths—for example, compassion, caring, curiosity, and courage—they develop a lexicon along with a new pattern for noticing these qualities. Student teachers have often shared anecdotally that they found themselves noticing and naming core qualities in *their* own students.

This excerpt came from a self-evaluation by a secondary science student teacher in the MAT (Master of Arts in Teaching) program who had just completed a course in Educational Foundations where core reflection was practiced.

> This is new territory for me, and while I feel a "drawing out" of the better parts of my nature taking place as I train to enter the profession, I fear that I won't have the personal strengths needed to surmount the brick wall of "reality" that I anticipate encountering shortly, or the conformity that it represents to me. . . . I was pleasantly surprised to be doing personal growth work in my [Foundations] course and grateful for the chance to think about my professional self from that uncomfortable space of vulnerability and honesty. It was a much-needed reminder that intentional, heart-centered work does not have to be relegated to sacred spaces held within my men's group, marriage, or family.

To the contrary, it will be desperately needed in my future classrooms and on my path as a teacher. (JS, summer 2012)

JS exemplifies a level of self-development that is possible within a single course where a transformative approach was integrated with the content of the course. Like many others, he makes the important connection between who he is as a person and who he wants to be as a teacher.

Using a series of intra- and interpersonal strategies, core reflection exercises were frequently used at the start of class to help students establish a sense of presence, connectedness, and calm. Over time, students realized that, rather than suppress or ignore the needs and longings of the soul, these courses would encourage such encounters.

Labyrinth

Another activity used for self-development in some of our courses is to build and walk a labyrinth. We began by introducing the metaphoric nature of labyrinths and ways they have been represented in other places around the world. Students share their own examples of labyrinth experiences and the symbolism an individual may encounter in a labyrinth. Then, in total silence, students work together with long sections of yarn (if indoors) or objects in nature (if outdoors) to construct a labyrinth of their own collective creation. As everyone stands encircling around the completed design, students are invited to remain open to the possibility of a more *spiritual* than perhaps *academic* experience.

Ceremoniously, we take turns entering and walking the labyrinth. After debriefing, one undergraduate described her experience this way in a written reflection:

> The labyrinth experience felt like an expanded version of every thought that goes through my mind. At first I leapt into analytical mode. . . . Next, I felt myself physically and emotionally step out of the activity for a moment to gain a greater vision for the perspectives of others. I realized that most of us were working from the outside in; I thought perhaps we need to start at the end (the center) . . . and how different life's experiences would be. (KK, February 2013)

This interpretation of her experience in the labyrinth suggests an encounter with something larger than her rational thought process. Kessler (2000) described the power of symbolic expression to engage more private parts of ourselves that we often protect from exposure. Perhaps KK had a glimpse of her own essence that appeared in her silent walk through the labyrinth.

Similarly, another student reacted to the labyrinth experience by revealing a new way of looking at his inner state:

> I realized while I was in the labyrinth that I had a deeper meaning and purpose in life than what I was allowing myself to have. I had many stories and experiences to tell that others could get insight from. I was not doing anyone any favors by remaining silent in all of my classes. Up until this class, I never spoke out in class. But this class and all of the experiences I had throughout the term showed me that it was time to let other people get to know the real JR. The labyrinth helped me sculpt my rite of passage. (JR, March 2015)

Comments like this open the door for whole class discussions about the value of these personal discoveries for their futures as teachers. The connections students discuss between the labyrinth and their future as teachers highlight key tenets of transformative teaching—namely, the integrated and dynamic nature of person, process, and curriculum. It is usually an easy connection for students to make, and once they do, such connections become a frequent topic for debriefings of other contemplative episodes.

Sometimes instead of providing a calming invitation to turn inward, the silence in the labyrinth can lead to uncomfortable feelings. In her reflection on the labyrinth activity, GG revealed the riskier side of teaching in the taboo:

> The labyrinth experience was hard for me. Being in silence in the class for so long was driving me crazy as it was. I wanted to yell and scream and cry. . . . I'm like Ariel from *The Little Mermaid*: I can't communicate that I'm drowning. (GG, February 2013)

Not all of GG's reactions to our contemplative experiences were negative; in fact, she liked most of them and garnered much respect from her classmates for her honesty and courage in expressing herself during debriefings. However, reactions such as hers brought forth a heightened sense of pedagogical tension within us as professors. Were we exposing our students to too much, too quickly? Had we crossed over into *taboo* areas in teacher preparation that placed too much emphasis on the *person* and not enough on the *theory* and *practice* of teaching?

These were, and still are, living questions for us. They give us pause, as they should, to consider each day, each student, and each decision in the classroom as significant when we invite encounters of a soulful nature with one another.

Personal Rite of Passage

The personal rite of passage is introduced in the Social Emotional Learning course. As a culminating project, it requires students to conceptualize and enact a rite of passage that symbolizes a milestone in their lives. Examples provided by Kessler (2000) outline three elements: separation, margin, and aggregation. Students incorporate all three when they design their own personal rite of passage.

Students are instructed that this project is a chance to connect to something within themselves that is, above all, meaningful to them at this point in time—perhaps a challenge they are facing, a painful time they wish to confront, a joy they want to celebrate, or a transition they are making in their lives. They enact their rite of passage outside of class; afterward, they summarize their experience in a class presentation and provide an activity that engages the group in one element or sensation involved in their personal rite. Rites have involved tattoos, name changing, sunrise vigils, *soul quests*, a letter of forgiveness to an absentee father, and a seven hundred-mile interstate road trip in silence to return to the scene of a childhood memory.

For some students who may have resisted becoming too exposed by opening up to the processes of self-awareness and contemplation offered to them each class, the rite of passage represented a final chance to immerse themselves in an experience of vulnerability and honesty. We may have no better example of this happening than in the story of KL, and it seems the best way to share this is to use her own words, captured at three different points in time, to tell her story. After eight weeks as a virtual nonparticipant in whole group class discussions, she finally opened up as the day for her rite of passage approached.

> This class was a struggle for me. I was terrified of letting my emotions spill out of me like water from a broken water balloon. The class dove into the deeper emotions an hour into our first class meeting. I was intimidated to say the least. In reflecting on the first weeks of class, I realized that I was standing on a wall between being open about my emotions, and hiding under a shy veil. I chose the latter. If it weren't for my fear of becoming vulnerable, I could have easily chosen the first option. (KL, Week 8, February 2015)

Her story continued the following week as she reflected on her upcoming rite of passage. She posted this on a shared class website:

> After exchanging a few heart-felt emails with [my instructor], I realized how much I've missed by not being more honest and open with you all. I wish I had the courage to share in the emotional conversations that have happened over these passed few weeks. . . . I don't know if I can be as "radically honest" as [another student] talked about on Monday, and I know I don't have the courage that [a different student] has, but I'd like to try. . . . I want to be vulnerable but I'm not sure how to be. I plan to explore this further in the coming week and in my rite of passage. (KL, Week 9, March 2015)

KL decided to hike alone to a small pond in the woods where she could gaze at her reflection in the water. Her period of marginality or liminality was to be "radically honest" and present with herself by describing what she saw in her reflection. In her final statement to the other students in the class, she shared this observation on our web page during the last week of the course:

> At first, I would get lost in my own chaotic and pressuring thoughts during times of silence and solitude. I would try too hard to look deep into my own soul and would become frustrated when I found nothing. I had to learn "silence and stillness" in my own way. I tried so hard to force it that I couldn't seem to get past myself to see what was inside me. . . . While at my destination for my rite of passage, I discovered solitude and eventually silence. I was able to relax. Enjoying the beauty around me I began to just be in the moment and let my own chaotic silence turn to just peace in my head. With this came a clarity that was not only refreshing, but necessary, like hydration to a dry, dying plant. . . . Of all the classes I have taken, this one has made the biggest impact on my life as woman, teacher, partner, and community member. (KL, Week 10, March 2015)

As our students prepare to transition from the teaching program to classrooms of their own, many are also transitioning away from their own schooling for the first time. Kessler (2000) wrote about the soul's hunger for initiation and for recognition of meaningful passages in one's life. Such passages are "not simply cognitive growth but changes to the core" (Kessler, 2000, p. 146).

KL's final reflection appears to represent more than a simple realization but a change to her identity, to the way she yearned to connect with herself. Without this experience, one wonders when in her own professional development she might discover this as a teacher? But perhaps the even larger goal of this activity is encouraging teachers to consider how such experiences might, as Kessler put it, *speak to the souls* of their future students.

CONCLUSION

Teachers and professors will not be prepared to meet the souls of their students and to guide them toward their potential as learners until they have encountered this potential in themselves. The voices in this chapter are a small but fairly representative sample of the hundreds we have heard over the past decade. They serve as reminders that, while teachers may feel like they are swimming against a current of status quo pedagogy, there are important reasons for balancing information and critical thinking with deeper and transformative encounters.

ESSENTIAL IDEAS TO CONSIDER

- Self-development matters as teachers and professors. When teacher candidates encounter personal revelations in their own learning, they begin to more clearly imagine how it might be to bring truly personal learning to the heads, hearts, and souls of their future students.
- Opening classroom curriculum to the uncharted realm of self-exploration requires professors to rethink their commitment to more transmissive styles of teaching and habits of pedagogy. Incorporating more time for personal connections and spaces for contemplation does not necessarily mean a sacrifice of content. In fact, it could promote more meaningful learning in ways that integrate rather than segregate knowledge.
- Soulful encounters inevitably produce feelings of vulnerability. Students will bring a diverse range of psychological conditioning to each risky new experience, and some will resist any invitation to expose themselves to others; it need not be forced. But, these students are becoming teachers, and by nurturing the kind of classroom culture where vulnerability can be introduced safely, lovingly, and gradually, the learning environment can become a place of trust, honesty, and a memorable touchstone as teacher candidates transition into leading classrooms of their own. In our classrooms, more often than not, poignant expressions of truth and emotional clarity emerge following activities that invite vulnerability and self-exploration.
- It only works when it's genuine. Instructors must be open to the same depths of self-discovery, vulnerability, and connectedness that they encourage in others. Students will sense the teacher's full presence and authenticity in modeling these attributes. Preparing for the awesome responsibility of transformative teaching means preparing oneself to enter the sacred space of the classroom and to lead with head, heart, *and* soul. Ultimately, transformative teaching and learning is, at its essence, an act of the spirit.

REFERENCES

Ayers, R., & Ayers, W. (2011). *Teaching the taboo: Courage and imagination in the classroom.* New York: Teachers College Press.

Intrator, S., & Kunzman, R. (2006). Starting with the soul. *Educational Leadership, 63*(6), 38–42.

Kessler, R. (2000). *The soul of education: Helping students find connection, compassion, and character at school.* Alexandria, VA: Association for Supervision and Curriculum Development.

Korthagen, F. A. J., Kim, Y. M., & Greene, W. L. (Eds.). (2013). *Teaching and learning from within: A core reflection approach to quality and inspiration in education.* New York/London: Routledge.

Korthagen, F. A. J., & Verkuyl, H. (2002). Do you meet your students or yourself? Reflection on professional identity as an essential component of teacher education. *Making a difference in teacher education through self-study* (2). Proceedings of the Fourth International Conference on Self-Study of Teacher Education Practices, Herstmonceux Castle, East Sussex, England. ISBN: 1-55339-025-3.

Miller, J. P. (2006). *Educating for wisdom and compassion: Creating conditions for timeless learning.* Thousand Oaks, CA: Corwin Press.

Miller, J. P. (2010). *Whole child education.* Toronto: University of Toronto Press.

Palmer, P. J. (1998). *The courage to teach: Exploring the inner landscape of a teacher's life.* San Francisco: Jossey-Bass.

Palmer, P. J. (2004). *A hidden wholeness: The journey toward an undivided life.* San Francisco: Jossey-Bass.

Chapter Two

Cultivating Mindful Teachers

Using a Mindfulness-Based Teaching Approach
with Student Teachers

Vanessa M. Villate and Gayle L. Butaud,
Lamar University, Beaumont, Texas

For many decades, research has shown the benefits of mindfulness for reducing stress, increasing well-being, and helping people become more present in their lives (Chiesa & Serretti, 2009; Grossman et al., 2004; Shapiro et al., 2011). Mindfulness-Based Stress Reduction (MBSR), a program initiated by Jon Kabat-Zinn in the 1970s, is recognized as a leader in the field of mindfulness. MBSR programs have been expanded from the initial focus on people suffering from chronic pain into other areas such as people with anxiety, as well as special populations such as prisoners, students, and health care workers.

In recent years, numerous programs that teach mindfulness in schools have been introduced to address the stress levels of both students and teachers. For example, the Garrison Institute initiated the CARE (Cultivating Awareness and Resilience in Education) program, a professional development program that includes thirty hours of intensive training over four to six weeks and has shown positive effects for teachers (Jennings et al., 2013). Some other courses available to teachers include Stress Management and Relaxation Techniques (SMART), PassageWorks' Soul of Education Program, and Mindful Schools, which offers online trainings (Roeser et al., 2012).

MINDFULNESS-BASED TEACHING APPROACH

Although an increasing number of teachers have access to learning about and incorporating mindfulness practices into their lives and into their teaching, many still do not have that opportunity. Dr. Lauren Alderfer developed a Mindfulness-Based Teaching Approach (MBTA) in 2015. The approach consists primarily of a reflective tool with the acronym HEARTS that guides teachers in considering classroom issues through a lens of mindfulness. The tool provides a tangible way for teachers to work with mindfulness practices in a structured format. A sample completed HEARTS form is shown in Table 2.1.

In using the HEARTS reflection, teachers begin by deciding which mindfulness quality they want to cultivate. Then, they complete the sections of the form that correspond to the acronym HEARTS: the H represents a *heartfelt* understanding of the mindfulness quality; the E is to *explain* the classroom challenge; the A is to *apply* the mindfulness quality intentionally; the R is to *review* appropriate classroom teaching strategies implemented; the T is to *take note of* student learning; and the S is to *self-reflect* for self-renewal and self-transformation.

For the study described in this chapter, the MBTA framework was utilized in dedicated mindfulness sessions with student teachers. The definition for mindfulness that guided this study was that of Kabat-Zinn (1990; 1994): "paying attention in a particular way; on purpose, in the present moment, and non-judgmentally" (p. 4). The research questions that steered the study were:

1. How does the MBTA ("HEARTS" form) impact the student teachers' work and their conception of teaching?
2. In what ways do the student teachers integrate the MBTA into their work?

To the researchers' knowledge, this is the first study to utilize the MBTA tool with teachers outside of Alderfer's own work developing the protocol. In particular, we were interested in how the use of the MBTA tool might help mitigate the student teachers' stress levels.

STRESS OF STUDENT TEACHERS

Learning to teach is a complex and multidimensional task that involves learning content, learning to teach, and self-growth. Many preservice teachers are not aware of the complexity of teaching and the myriad other issues that are encountered in the classroom: classroom management, understand-

Table 2.1. Sample HEARTS Form

Mindfulness Quality
What quality or ethical value do I want to cultivate?
_____*patience*_____

Heartfelt understanding of the mindfulness quality	H	How can I explain this quality in my own words? *The sense of endurance under stressful situations.*
Explain the classroom challenge	E	What is the classroom issue I am facing? *There are so many things that teachers have to face throughout their day. I like to have a pretty good handle on situations. Right now, though, I don't feel that I have much control of my surroundings. I was finding it hard to adjust to the lack of control.*
Apply the mindfulness quality intentionally	A	How do I integrate the mindfulness quality in what I do or what the student does? *I had to focus on being patient throughout my day. I had to remind myself often during instruction to breathe and be more patient.*
Review appropriate classroom teaching strategies implemented	R	What specific techniques, learning strategies, or activities will I implement? *I have tried to step back and breathe more. Also, I have tried to think before I act. I feel that being more aware of my actions will drastically change my response to situations.*
Take note of student learning	T	What were the results in student learning? *Now, I catch myself and remind myself to take time to respond to situations. This, in turn, brings about more confidence with the students when they approach me.*
Self-reflect for self-renewal and self-transformation	S	How has this mindfulness quality been further cultivated in me? How have I changed? What are any next steps? *I have gotten a better hold on all of the chaos that marks a teacher's school day. The students and I are having more positive interactions in the classroom.*

HEARTS—A Mindfulness-Based Teaching Approach (MBTA)
The HEARTS form first appeared in *Teaching from the Heart of Mindfulness* Copyright © Lauren Alderfer, PhD, published by Green Writers Press 2015. Used by permission.

ing the ways students learn, assessment practices, and working with colleagues (Lee, 2008; Miller, 2008).

The learning that takes place in the university is often out of context from the learning that the preservice teachers experience in the public school classroom (Lave & Wenger, 1991; Smagorinsky et al., 2004; Zeichner, 2010).

The classroom mentor may know very little about the specific methods and theories in coursework the student teacher has completed at the university, and university supervisors may know very little about the instructional strategies and culture of the P–12 classroom where preservice teachers are placed (Caires, Almeida, & Vieira, 2012).

Preservice teachers are stressed by a maelstrom of expectations, coming from both the outside world (the university) and the inside world (the classroom) (Smagorinsky et al., 2004; Zeichner, 2010). Trying to meet the expectations of both the university and mentor teacher can be confusing and discouraging (Merc, 2010; Zeichner, 2010). Preservice teachers may find that mentor teachers' practice does not match the teaching skills studied at the university, creating friction for the preservice teacher seeking to follow a philosophy developed through coursework at the university level (Smagorinsky et al., 2004; Stuart & Thurlow, 2000).

Blending in with the environment rather than expanding on the teaching strategies and tools learned at the university may be a result of the preservice teacher trying to meet the mentor teacher's expectation in planning, grading, and taking on the teacher role (Smagorinsky et al., 2004). Further negotiating on the preservice teachers' part is created when the supervisors observe teaching with a strong emphasis on criticism. The preservice teacher is unlikely to take a risk to expand on the knowledge learned in the classroom and coursework (Darling-Hammond, 2006).

These demands and negotiating efforts can leave preservice teachers feeling inadequate, stretched, and questioning their choice of careers. Providing preservice teachers with a reflective tool, such as the HEARTS form, to guide mindfulness can possibly reduce the stress felt as a new teacher and create teaching from a present frame of mind (Chiesa & Serretti, 2009; Grossman et al., 2004; Shapiro et al., 2011).

METHODOLOGY

The participants for this study were the forty-five student teachers who were enrolled in the student teaching seminar in the fall of 2015 at a regional university in southeast Texas. The undergraduate program in the College of Education and Human Development certifies teachers in all grade levels and a variety of disciplines. Student teaching is the culminating experience in students' educational programs.

In addition to their teaching responsibilities at a local pre-K–12 school during the semester, student teachers were required to attend six full-day seminars on the university campus. The seminars provided professional development in areas of teaching, education, and job seeking. All student teachers met together as one group, which included student teachers from all grade levels and disciplines. During each of these seminars, the researchers facilitated a thirty-minute mindfulness session, conducted in person. The mindfulness session took place in the middle of the seminar day, just before the lunch break.

In the first session, a pre-study survey was given, which consisted of four open-ended questions about the students' experience with mindfulness: 1) What do you think is the most important quality (or qualities) for you to embody as a teacher? 2) What is your experience with mindfulness (or other contemplative practices, such as yoga)? 3) How do you think mindfulness could help you personally? and, 4) How do you think mindfulness could help you with your teaching placement? This was followed by a five-minute guided breath meditation and a ten-minute small-group reflection on the experience.

The second session began with a five-minute guided meditation and then the Mindfulness-Based Teaching Approach (MBTA), the HEARTS form, was introduced. Students completed a sample HEARTS form based on a teaching vignette read by the researchers. The teaching vignette was from a chapter in Alderfer's (2015) *Teaching from the Heart of Mindfulness*. This was done so that the student teachers could become acquainted with the HEARTS form as originally designed.

The format for the third through fifth sessions was the same: a five- to ten-minute guided, seated meditation; reflection in small groups about how they were using mindfulness practices in their personal and professional lives; and ten to fifteen minutes to complete a HEARTS form of their own, choosing a different mindfulness quality each time and reflecting on a classroom challenge from their current teaching placement.

In the sixth session, students again were guided through a ten-minute seated meditation, followed by small-group reflections. Then they completed the post-study survey, which consisted of seven open-ended questions: 1) What do you think is the most important quality (or qualities) for you to embody as a teacher? Why? 2) How do you think mindfulness has helped you personally? 3) How do you think mindfulness has helped you with your teaching placement? 4) To what extent did you utilize the mindfulness-based teaching approaches ("HEARTS") in your teaching? 5) How did it impact what you did on a daily basis? 6) How has it impacted your ideas about teaching? and 7) Other thoughts related to mindfulness practices?

Data for this study consisted of 1) the answers to pre- and post-study open-ended survey questions about their experiences with mindfulness and how they were able to integrate the practices into their lives; and 2) the students' three completed HEARTS forms. The researchers compiled all responses to the questions from the surveys, as well as the focus of each completed HEARTS form, in an Excel spreadsheet. The data was analyzed qualitatively, as described by Merriam (1998), and the constant comparative method of theme generation was utilized to discover trends (Glaser & Strauss, 1967).

In order to answer the two research questions, the data was categorized by which research question it addressed. To answer the first question, "How does the MBTA ("HEARTS" form) impact the student teachers' work and their conception of teaching?," the responses to the questions on the pre-study and post-study surveys were compared and analyzed.

To answer the second question, "In what ways do the student teachers integrate the MBTA into their work?," the completed HEARTS forms were analyzed. Information from the HEARTS forms that was analyzed included the mindfulness quality chosen and the nature of the challenge (teacher-focused or student-focused).

FINDINGS

The results of the study are divided into three sections based on the research questions. The first section, *impact on student teachers' work*, describes how they utilized the MBTA and mindfulness practices on a daily basis. The second section, *conception of teaching*, describes how the student teachers' perceptions of teaching were changed by the MBTA and mindfulness practices. Finally, the third section, *integration into work*, describes what the students included on their HEARTS forms.

Impact on Student Teachers' Work

A large majority of participants (thirty-five of the forty-five students) noted that the mindfulness practices helped them in their teaching placement to be more focused, centered, calm, and positive. For example, in response to the question on the final survey, "How do you think mindfulness has helped you with your teaching placement?," one participant wrote, "I apply mindfulness when I feel overwhelmed in the classroom. I take 2 minutes and [do] not do or say anything to regain strength and stay focused."

Another commented, "It helps me keep calm and be present in that moment and not think about tomorrow." Other comments included, "It gave me patience to help students," "It helped me feel more positive and calm," and "It's taught me to be present with my students . . . during breaks, I can worry about all of my work." One other student wrote, "I sometimes used the mindfulness techniques to calm down anxious children. It also helped me create a yoga activity where the students were learning at the same time."

Another post-study survey question about the impact on their work was "To what extent did you utilize the mindfulness-based teaching approaches ("HEARTS") in your teaching?" Perhaps because of their newness to mindfulness practices (only six of the forty-five students noted any prior experience with contemplative practices), most of the student teachers seemed to equate the MBTA with mindfulness practices in general.

The most telling comment in response to the survey question was, "Not the HEARTS form, but the principles, often. It helped me reflect on what I did, how it worked, and what needs to change."

However, the intent of using the MBTA tool for this study was to teach mindfulness practices in a tangible way and for students to integrate mindfulness into their teaching. Therefore, most definitely, the results showed that it impacted the student teachers' work and their conception of teaching, and forty out of the forty-five participants did report integrating it into their work. To this end, one participant commented, "Mindfulness has helped me remain calm under stressful situations. It has helped me develop patience with my students."

Other student teacher comments included, "I would just stop and breathe every time I felt stressed," "If there was a difficult situation, I would take a deep breath and think about the problem," and "I used the breathing techniques between classes and during stressful times." These comments indicate that the slower breathing used with mindfulness meditation practice had a significant impact on the student teachers and that they used it frequently during the day.

In response to the end of semester survey question, "How did it (MBTA/mindfulness) impact what you did on a daily basis?," over half of the participants (thirty of the forty-five students) noted the calmness and presence they felt because of the practices. For example, one participant wrote, "It taught me to be fully present wherever I am." Another student teacher commented, "It helped me focus on each class period instead of worrying about the next one" and "It helped me leave work behind when going home."

Conception of Teaching

In the surveys given at the beginning of the semester and again at the end of the semester, student teachers were asked, "What do you think is the most important quality (or qualities) for you to embody as a teacher?" Early in the semester, sixteen participants included *patience* in their response; other identified qualities included organization, consistency, passion about content area, and dedication. Most student teachers listed three qualities.

At the end of the semester, most of them only listed one quality and the number of references to *patience* increased to twenty-eight. Other top qualities identified were calmness (four students), compassion (three students), and love (three students). The student teachers seemed to have realized the importance of the human relational and support aspects of teaching, in part due to teaching full-time, as well as the influence of the mindfulness practices.

Another way that the researchers sought to understand how the mindfulness sessions impacted student teachers' conception of teaching was by asking on the final survey, "How has it (mindfulness/MBTA) impacted your ideas about teaching?" Responses to this question were divided into two main areas. The first area, which comprised fifteen of the forty-five responses, included how mindfulness can also help P–12 students, especially, as one student teacher wrote, "The students go through stressful situations as well and they could use mindfulness in their day, too." Other comments included, "It's made me more aware of how I can help my students calm down" and "It reminded me to give students time to think and be calm before class begins."

The second area, which comprised twenty-five of the forty-five responses, was how mindfulness can decrease the stress levels of teaching. One participant noted, "We should learn how to cope to be better teachers." Other comments included, "All teachers should go through mindfulness exercises," "I now see that, to be an effective teacher, you have to embrace the 'now' as well as remain calm," and "It's given me a better perspective, seeing the bigger picture." The remaining five participants cited both benefit areas; for example, one student teacher wrote, "the students are stressed out just like the teachers."

Integration into their Work

In order to answer the second research question, "In what ways do the student teachers integrate the MBTA into their work?," the focus is specifically on the HEARTS forms that the student teachers completed during the semester. The researchers analyzed the forms based on two of the letter categories: 1) the A, "*Apply* the mindfulness quality intentionally"; and 2) the R, "*Review* appropriate classroom teaching strategies implemented."

The participants submitted a total of eighty-eight HEARTS forms at the end of the semester. As designed by Alderfer, the first step in completing the HEARTS form is to identify a mindfulness quality to cultivate. Top qualities that participants chose included patience (twenty-one times), calmness (seventeen times), acceptance (fifteen times), focus (seven times), compassion (six times), and kindness (four times). The ways in which they applied the mindfulness qualities differed by topic. Due to space limitations, only representative responses from the top two mindfulness qualities are included here.

For patience, applications included:

• Trying not to get overwhelmed and allow the students time to fix the problem.
• Trying to be patient so not to get aggravated with this class.

- Taking a step away for a few moments and taking ten deep breaths.

For calmness, applications included:

- I stop and think before I act. I also remain calm and take a deep breath.
- When I see his attitude start to become angry, I stand beside him and tell him he's doing well and to breathe.
- Take a step back, evaluate the actual situation and regroup.

Specific techniques and teaching strategies also differed by topic. For patience, strategies that participants used included:

- I could take a break to gather my thoughts and allow myself to calm down before handling a situation or talking to the student.
- I try to separate the more disruptive students in this class.
- I would practice this activity with my student once a day so we can all learn to be more patient with everyone.

For calmness, teaching strategies included:

- To teach my students to stop and think about their behaviors before they do them, and model how to remain calm and take deep breaths when needed.
- By having him look at me and breathe it seems to bring him back.
- Refraining from allowing minor setbacks to control the entire tone of the classroom.

One student teacher used the same classroom issue in two of her forms but realized that a different quality was needed. The situation she described was students making fun of foreign exchange students. She began to address it through discussions with her students about professionalism; however, she realized that compassion was a more effective quality in overcoming the challenge. All of these examples indicate the extent to which the student teachers integrated mindfulness and the MBTA into their work.

DISCUSSION

Overall, the data from this study indicated that the student teachers enjoyed learning mindfulness practices and utilizing them in their teaching. The results of this study were similar to Dorman's (2015) descriptions of the majority of students expressing contentment with learning mindfulness practices and their perceived usefulness for their personal and professional lives, as well as very few expressing dislike of the time spent in the mindfulness sessions. Participants' reports of lowered stress levels and an increased ability to be present to their students corroborate Bernay's (2014) findings with novice teachers utilizing mindfulness practices.

From a pedagogical perspective, one main issue was encountered with using the MBTA HEARTS form. The issue was that, on the form, the first item students were supposed to choose was the mindfulness quality. This would have been easier if students had previous experience with mindfulness practices. However, almost none of the participants had prior experience, so they struggled with that first step. Once this gap was realized, students were asked to begin with a classroom issue and then think of a mindfulness quality that could be helpful. As novice teachers, they certainly had no problem thinking of classroom issues.

CONCLUSION

To help students avoid becoming overwhelmed with the stresses that are inherent in the student teaching semester, teacher educators could provide opportunities for preservice teachers to learn skills of incorporating mindfulness practices into their personal lives and into their teaching lives. Regular emphasis across the teacher preparation program aimed at mindfulness activities could lead preservice teachers to a more focused, centered, and calm student teaching experience as boundaries and tensions are being explored in this demanding semester.

Providing coping strategies could decrease student teachers' stress levels and increase their self-esteem and feelings of competence. Through their own practice of mindfulness, preservice teachers can impart the practice of being present in each moment and teaching more authentically to their own students. The Mindfulness-Based Teaching Approach (MBTA) as designed by Alderfer (2015) seems to be an effective way to initiate conversations about mindfulness and allow preservice teachers the opportunity to find ways of integrating mindfulness into their work.

ESSENTIAL IDEAS TO CONSIDER

- Student teachers are particularly vulnerable to stress as they are pulled between their campus teaching assignment and the university requirements.
- The Mindfulness-Based Teaching Approach (MBTA) tool seems to be an effective and concrete way to introduce mindfulness perspectives to student teachers.

- Mindfulness practice sessions facilitated for student teachers were helpful for them to learn how to center themselves and stay focused and, in turn, to help their students do the same.

REFERENCES

Alderfer, L. (2015). *Teaching from the heart of mindfulness.* Brattleboro, VT: Green Writers Press.

Bernay, R. S. (2014). Mindfulness and the beginning teacher. *Australian Journal of Teacher Education, 39*(7), 58–69.

Caires, S., Almeida, L., & Vieira, D. (2012). Becoming a teacher: Student teachers' experiences and perceptions about teaching practice. *European Journal of Teacher Education, 35*(2), 163–178.

Chiesa, A., & Serretti, A. (2009). Mindfulness-based stress reduction for stress management in healthy people: A review and meta-analysis. *Journal of Alternative and Complementary Medicine, 15*(5), 593–600.

Darling-Hammond, L. (2006). Constructing 21st-century teacher education. *Journal of Teacher Education, 57*(3), 300–314.

Dorman, E. H. (2015). Building teachers' social-emotional competence through mindfulness practices. *Curriculum and Teaching Dialogue, 17*(1), 103–119.

Glaser, B. G., & Strauss, A. (1967). *Discovery of grounded theory: Strategies for qualitative research.* Chicago: Aldine.

Grossman, P., Niemann, L., Schmidt, S., & Walach, H. (2004). Mindfulness-based stress reduction and health benefits: A meta-analysis. *Journal of Psychosomatic Research, 57*(1), 35–43.

Jennings, P. A., Frank, J. L., Snowberg, K. E., Coccia, M. A., & Greenberg, M. T. (2013). Improving classroom learning environments by cultivating awareness and resilience in education (CARE): Results of a randomized controlled trial. *School Psychology Quarterly, 28*(4), 374–390.

Kabat-Zinn, J. (1990). *Full catastrophe living.* New York: Bantam.

Kabat-Zinn, J. (1994). *Wherever you go, there you are.* New York: Hyperion.

Lave, J., & Wenger, E. (1991). *Situated learning: Legitimate peripheral participation.* Cambridge, MA: Cambridge University Press.

Lee, I. (2008). Fostering preservice reflection through response journals. *Teacher Education Quarterly, 35*(1), 117–139.

Merc, A. (2010). Self-reported problems of pre-service EFL teachers throughout teaching practicum. *Anadolu University Journal of Social Sciences, 10*(2), 199–226.

Merriam, S. (1998). *Qualitative research and case study applications in education.* San Francisco: Jossey-Bass.

Miller, M. (2008). Problem-based conversations: Using preservice teachers' problems as a mechanism for their professional development. *Teacher Education Quarterly, 35*(4), 77–98.

Roeser, R. W., Skinner, E., Beers, J., & Jennings, P. A. (2012). Mindfulness training and teachers' professional development: An emerging area of research and practice. *Child Development Perspectives, 6*(2), 167–173.

Shapiro, S. L., Brown, K. W., Thoresen, C., & Plante, T. G. (2011). The moderation of mindfulness-based stress reduction effects by trait mindfulness: Results from a randomized controlled trial. *Journal of Clinical Psychology, 67*(3), 267–277. doi:10.1002/jclp.20761.

Smagorinsky, P., Cook, L. S., Moore, C., Jackson, A. Y., & Fry, P. G. (2004). Tensions in learning to teach: Accommodation and the development of a teaching identity. *Journal of Teacher Education, 55*(1), 8–24. doi:10.1177/0022487103260067.

Stuart, C., & Thurlow, D. (2000). Making it their own: Pre-service teachers' experiences, beliefs, and classroom practices. *Journal of Teacher Education, 51*(2), 113–121.

Zeichner, K. M. (2010). Rethinking the connections between campus courses and field experiences in college- and university-based teacher education. *Educação Santa Maria, 35*(3), 479–501.

Chapter Three

Cultivating Reflective Teaching Practice through Mindfulness

Evan E. Moss, Matthew J. Hirshberg, Lisa Flook,
and M. Elizabeth Graue,
University of Wisconsin–Madison,
Madison, Wisconsin

LANDSCAPE OF REFLECTION IN TEACHER EDUCATION

Teaching is more than the cognitive application of learned technical knowledge and skills (Fairbanks et al., 2009). It is a complex, evolving, and demanding practice. Inherently social, effective teaching requires deep engagement with not just one's students but also one's internal world of thoughts and emotions. Therefore, maintaining reflective teaching as an anchoring practice and core principle within teacher education programs is critical.

Yet, despite the ubiquity of "reflective teaching" nomenclature within teacher education, there exists no consensus definition (Hatton & Smith, 1995) nor a validated method for cultivating reflective capacity. Moreover, reflection is commonly taught as a technical, cognitive strategy for improving pedagogy with the goal of enhancing student achievement.

In this chapter, we reconstruct reflective practice to encompass "mindful reflection" or present-moment centered awareness characterized by openness and equanimity. Redefined in this way, we propose that reflective practice will allow teachers to better understand and regulate their assumptions, motivations, affect, and cognitions, supporting teacher well-being and student achievement.

A CASE FOR REFLECTION

Teaching is an emotional practice. Hargreaves (1998) argues, "Good teachers are not just well-oiled machines. They are emotional, passionate beings who connect with their students and fill their work and their classes with pleasure, creativity, challenge, and joy" (p. 835). The potential downside to the deeply emotional work of teaching is that when challenges arise, optimism, hope, and positive aspirations may transform into stress and feelings of being overwhelmed, ultimately resulting in burnout. Indeed, stress levels are alarmingly high, especially among new teachers (American Psychological Association, "Teacher Stress Module," 2013). Attrition rates are close to 50 percent after five years of teaching (Ingersoll & Merrill, 2012).

It is increasingly clear that the quality of teacher-student relationships is critically important to student development and achievement. Teacher-student relationships that are characterized as warm and supportive predict school performance as well as social-emotional adjustment (Osher et al., 2008), even serving as a protective factor against the development of depression during adolescence (Wang, Brinkworth, & Eccles, 2013).

In contrast, detached or conflict-ridden student-teacher relationships, symptomatic of distressed and burnt-out teachers, predict academic underachievement in the short-term and longitudinally (Spilt et al., 2012) as well as student aggression (Howes, Hamilton, & Matheson, 1994).

While a degree of mindful reflection may be intrinsic in some individuals, others do not inherently possess *as much of* this capacity. Without intentional development of mindful reflection, these teachers' ability to foster supportive relationships with students may be compromised, enhancing stress and reducing well-being. Teacher education programs currently lack a systematic approach to develop this capacity.

One of the most common and difficult transitions that teachers make is moving from concerns about the self, such as a focus on self-adequacy, to concerns about the other (Feiman–Nemser, 2012). When preservice teachers actually confront the realities of teaching, there may be a tendency to seek basic survival skills at the expense of a deeper understanding of the complex interplay between teachers and students and teaching and learning (Kitchen, 2005). Indeed, during student teaching, preservice teachers tend to mimic a cooperating teacher's often more traditional style, picking up conservative practices and focusing more on how to control students rather than on student learning (Rozelle & Wilson, 2012).

Whereas preservice teachers may have been socialized to see teaching as simple, they are faced with complexity, competing demands, and dilemma-ridden situations (Fairbanks et al., 2009). Ball and Cohen's (1999) notion that "teaching occurs in particulars—particular students interacting with particular teachers over particular ideas in particular circumstances" (p. 10) highlights the impossibility of preparing preservice teachers for the infinitely variable situations they will encounter. No body of knowledge can prescribe the "right" practice for each moment, but cultivating mindful reflection will allow for adaptive responding.

In summary, teacher well-being and student achievement are intimately related through the quality of teacher-student relationships and the classroom learning environment. Mindful reflection, or the quality of reflective practice developed through mindfulness training, can support teacher well-being and pedagogy, allowing for in-the-moment reflection of the infinite "particulars."

By cultivating this capacity in preservice teachers, two problems in contemporary education may be substantially addressed: teacher stress leading to teacher turnover, and suboptimal teacher-student relationships resulting in a degraded learning environment.

DEFINING REFLECTIVE TEACHING

John Dewey's (1933) conceptualization of reflection provides the foundation for most current uses of the term. Calderhead (1989) captures the essence of Dewey's words in his description of reflection as a "purposeful, reasoned search for a solution" and "initiated by uncertainty and guided by one's conception of a goal or end-point" (p. 44). This approach to fostering reflective capabilities in teachers seeks to develop strengths of observation, analysis, interpretation, and decision making (Zeichner & Liston, 2013). Based on this idea of reflection, current models of teaching reflection are highly technical, relying on methods of problem solving and encouraging linear thought processes (Tremmel, 1993).

Recent changes in the public narrative of education have also influenced contemporary notions of reflective practice. As the landscape of K–12 education has marched toward greater emphasis on accountability by way of high-stakes testing, the role of reflection has further solidified around a technical, outcome-oriented conceptualization. In response to federal law (e.g., No Child Left Behind), student achievement became narrowly defined by standardized test scores. When achievement is defined by standardized knowledge, the pressure for classroom pedagogy to reorient toward scripted curricula, canonical knowledge dissemination, and formulaic, test-driven instruction grows (Au, 2007).

It is not uncommon in contemporary schools and classrooms to approach reflection under the goal of data-informed decision making. To be clear, data-informed decision making is important for effective instruction. However, a myopic focus on "the data" (i.e., standardized assessment scores) loses sight of critical thinking and inquiry on the part of students and tends to push instruction toward replicable, scripted behaviors that leave little room for mindful reflection.

REFLECTION ON ACTION VERSUS REFLECTION IN ACTION

Loughran's (1995) reflective framework delineates three types of reflection: anticipatory reflection, contemporaneous reflection, and retrospective reflection. Anticipatory reflection happens during the planning process as the practitioner thinks about what they anticipate happening in their lesson, contemporaneous reflection entails the "on the spot" decisions made while teaching, and retrospective reflection happens when thinking about the lesson afterward. Most teacher education programs approach cultivating reflective skills through processes of anticipatory and retrospective reflection.

Activities designed to encourage preservice teachers to think about their practice can include microteaching, free and journal writing, dialogic reflection, and action research (Hatton & Smith, 1995). Typical reflective questions asked by preservice teachers such as "How well did I teach?," "What assumptions have I made in teaching this way?," and "How else might I have taught the lesson?" are likewise retrospective in nature. Interestingly, even dialogue about "on the spot" or contemporaneous reflection usually occurs retrospectively (Freese, 1999).

While anticipatory and retrospective reflective processes are valuable to teacher development, contemporaneous reflection is paramount but least emphasized. Classroom climate and teacher-student relationship quality can be benefited or harmed by a momentary decision, and no level of anticipation or retrospective reflection can rewind these spur-of-the-moment actions.

In the absence of targeted training to develop such capacity, we question the degree to which anticipatory and retrospective reflection supports contemporaneous reflection or the capacity for mindful reflection (see Calderhead, 1989). Indeed, substantial social science research demonstrates that it is precisely in times of high emotionality and stress that human beings are least capable of reflection and self-regulation (e.g., Muraven & Baumeister, 2000). Moreover, stress and high emotionality are ubiquitous in teaching.

Mindful reflection is a skill that affords teachers the presence of mind to become aware of and respond adaptively to their unfolding external and internal environments. For example, mindful reflection (i.e., contemporaneous reflection) may allow a teacher to notice the early somatic, cognitive, and emotional indicators of frustration and impatience. This noticing may be sufficient for a teacher to then regulate an impulsive, reactive behavior that could serve to damage student-teacher dynamics and the classroom climate as a whole.

Similarly, reflective capacity might emerge as an awareness of the class-room environment. This moment-to-moment information may impact the quality of attention given to students and inform instruction so that pedagogy is tailored to the present, not just the anticipated, needs of students.

In summary, we have identified three main problems with current concep-tualizations of reflective teaching. First, reflective practice has often been reduced to a cognitive, technical evaluation of pedagogy with the goal of improving a narrow, standardized notion of student achievement.

Second, reflective practice has lost sight of the critical importance of the internal world of the teacher to classroom climate, pedagogy, and ultimately student achievement. As a consequence, preservice teachers receive little to no training in negotiating the stress, doubt, and strong emotions that attend to teaching (Jennings & Greenberg, 2009).

Third, the scope of reflective practice must be broadened so that reflec-tion can be applied in-the-moment. From this perspective, reflection is more than a linear thought process, but rather a suite of skills (e.g., present-cen-tered awareness, equanimity) that allow teachers to skillfully respond to the particulars of teaching.

CULTIVATING REFLECTIVE TEACHING PRACTICE THROUGH MINDFULNESS

Mindful reflection consists of a loose constellation of *inter*personal and *intra*personal skills. Intrapersonal skills comprise those capacities that one calls upon when noticing and working with thoughts, emotions, and reac-tions. Interpersonal skills are capacities, often representative of intrapersonal skills, which emerge as one interacts with students, colleagues, and others in the educational environment. The foundation of these skills is basic aware-ness.

The first step in building mindful reflection is to become more sensitive and attuned to one's internal (e.g., thoughts, emotions, sensations) and exter-nal (e.g., classroom environment, students) experience, which are seamlessly interconnected (Byrnes, 2012).

For instance, to respond to the needs of students, a teacher must first be aware of the need. This may include awareness of aspects of the individual student (e.g., emotional state), awareness of classroom and interpersonal dy-namics, and awareness of the student's prior knowledge or schema. Similar-ly, in order to effectively manage stress and frustration, a teacher must first be aware that such feelings are present.

However, simply becoming aware of a student need or one's own stress is not sufficient. Indeed, awareness of the former without the flexibility to alter instruction in some way to benefit the student will not satisfy the need. In the latter case, awareness of stress, anxiety, or other negative emotionality may only serve to reinforce it, especially when these feelings are accompanied by perseverative thinking or self-doubt (e.g., Nolen-Hoeksema, 2000). In fact, experiencing strong negative emotions while lacking the capacity to effectively regulate them is descriptive of the syndrome of burnout (Maslach, Schaufeli, & Leiter, 2001).

Mindfulness is ubiquitously characterized as "the awareness that emerges through paying attention on purpose, in the present moment, and nonjudgmentally to the unfolding of experience" (Kabat-Zinn, 2003, p. 145). Awareness is central to mindfulness. In particular, mindfulness training is intended to cultivate awareness imbued with equanimity. Equanimity is the capacity to be with experience as it arises, without reactively being swayed by the content of experience. For example, a teacher who has cultivated equanimity may experience tension in the body as frustration arises, but that embodied frustration is allowed to be fully experienced.

In contrast, resistance enhances frustration. In addition to the unpleasant feeling, resistance adds a layer of not wanting what is present. The more the feeling persists, the greater the resistance, the more negative the experience becomes. It is during resistance that a teacher is most likely to become so overwhelmed that she lashes out at students in anger.

Equanimity provides a "workspace" in which response rather than reaction to experience can occur (e.g., Vago & Silbersweig, 2012). This workspace is a necessary ingredient for mindful reflection. It allows teachers to flexibly adapt instructional or management behaviors so that they meet the needs of the student(s) in front of them. Although mindfulness in education research is in its infancy, there exists preliminary support for this contention (e.g., Flook et al., 2013; Roeser et al., 2013).

Techniques for building this workspace are lacking in current teacher education programs. Mindfulness is a method well suited to building the foundation of mindful reflection. For example, body-scan practice, a core mindfulness training, trains the mind to be aware and accepting of the whole spectrum of bodily sensations.

As in our example of equanimity above, body-scan practice can provide an alternative approach to working with difficult (and positive) emotions so that one experiences but is not driven by them. It is not surprising then that among the most robust effects of mindfulness training are reductions in negative affect (e.g., Goyal et al., 2014).

Stress and feeling overwhelmed are common experiences for preservice and new teachers (American Psychological Association, "Teacher Stress Module," 2013). These states tend to narrow awareness to perception of only one's negative experience (Ayduk & Kross, 2010), limiting the capacity to perceive others fully and reducing well-being (Lo, Ho, & Hollon, 2010) thereby threatening key constituents of effective teaching (e.g., student-teacher relationship quality). Cultivating mindfulness in preservice teachers has the potential to support a host of salutary skills: effective regulation of emotion, resilience to stress, enhanced awareness of others, and increased kindness (Condon et al., 2013).

Enhanced awareness coupled with equanimity toward experience provides new opportunities to notice the needs of others. This enhanced noticing opens the door to higher quality relationships with students as well as matching instruction to student needs. A major benefit of developing these skills during preservice teacher education is that mindful reflection can become a primary disposition, providing a foundation of resiliency before it is called upon.

Mindfulness may be a powerful support for enhancing preservice teacher education, but it is not a panacea. Although little empirical work has been conducted on individual differences in response to mindfulness training, it is clear that mindfulness training does not produce uniform results. Some individuals benefit more and others less. The factors contributing to these differences remain to be explicated, but motivation, time dedicated to mindfulness practice, and the quality of the curriculum and instructors are likely contributors (Davidson & Kaszniak, 2015).

Integrating mindfulness or other contemplative practices (e.g., compassion) into preservice teacher education will likely require several iterations before the curriculum is optimized. Our experience has been that explicitly integrating teaching-related experiences into the mindfulness training enhances engagement and interest in the training.

Another area of concern is the ever-broadening scope of activities described as mindfulness. We use the term to reflect contemplative techniques derived from long-standing contemplative traditions. Mindfulness-Based Stress Reduction (Kabat-Zinn, 1982) is currently paradigmatic, but other programs exist meeting this criterion. Relatedly, we are wary of curricula offering a quick fix.

Mindfulness and other contemplative training regimens are traditionally thought to produce benefits over time (Davidson & Kaszniak, 2015). Although research on mindfulness has not come to a consensus on optimal duration and intensity of training, in general, more practice seems to predict stronger results. Because preservice teacher education typically occurs over several semesters, integrating mindfulness training into it has the potential benefit of offering extended exposure to mindfulness.

In the novel well-being training our group has developed and is currently researching with preservice teachers, mindfulness is one of several qualities the program is intended to foster. First, practices intended to cultivate attention, equanimity, and meta-awareness are introduced (Dahl, Lutz, & Davidson, 2015). Clarifying and then strengthening the intention and motivation to teach are important elements of the training.

Also infused are kindness and compassion, practices that can direct the attention cultivated through mindfulness in prosocial ways. The hope is that when a preservice teacher experiences reactivity, they will engage mindful reflection, which could include remembering (a classical definition of mindfulness) the motivation that drove them to teach, thereby opening a workspace in which emerges a response based on caring motivation instead of reactive frustration.

The training is designed explicitly to engage preservice teachers' teaching experiences. Several strategies are used to achieve this, including asking preservice teachers to reflect on a successful or challenging teaching experience as the basis for exploration during a mindfulness practice. Preservice teachers may be "assigned" an informal practice of simply taking a brief moment before entering the classroom to recall and deeply feel the caring motivation that led them to teaching.

Qualitative reports from preservice teachers suggest they are putting mindful reflection into practice. One participant described the challenges she faces working with students with behavioral difficulties. In her school, the term "red zone" is used to describe behavior that has elevated to the point of being highly disruptive.

Prior to engaging a student who often enters the red zone, this preservice teacher spontaneously recalled an informal check-in practice where one very quickly scans sensations in the body as well as the quality of mind. She did this practice immediately before engaging this student and discovered that she was nearly entering the red zone herself in anticipation of what might happen. She went on to explain how this awareness helped her maintain more balance so that she was receptive to the student instead of reacting to him based on her own anticipation of how the interaction would unfold.

CONCLUSION

Scholarship on teacher education has long emphasized the importance of reflection in teaching. What has been largely absent, however, are effective strategies for developing the mode of reflection that will have the greatest impact on preservice and professional teachers: mindful reflection.

Cultivating mindfulness, through carefully curated contemplative curricula, can help solve the gap between knowing and actualizing by furnishing preservice teachers with the inter- and intrapersonal skills required for contemporaneous or mindful reflection. As mindfulness and other contemplative techniques gain traction in teacher education and elsewhere, it is critical that careful consideration be given to the skills that enable teachers and students to flourish, and the practice or practices best suited to the cultivation of those skills.

ESSENTIAL IDEAS TO CONSIDER

- The inner life of the teacher deserves recognition and support.
- The approach to fostering reflective capacities within teacher education programs is currently limited.
- Mindful reflection can support teacher well-being and pedagogy. It is a skill that can be learned through practice.
- Mindful reflection is present-moment centered awareness characterized by openness and equanimity.
- Many of the qualities of effective teachers can be developed through mindfulness training.

REFERENCES

American Psychological Association. (2013). Teacher stress module. Accessed on April 23, 2015, at http://www.apa.org/ed/schools/cpse/activities/teacher-stress.aspx.

Au, W. (2007). High-stakes testing and curricular control: A qualitative metasynthesis. *Educational Researcher, 36*(5), 258–267.

Ayduk, Ö., & Kross, E. (2010). From a distance: Implications of spontaneous self–distancing for adaptive self-reflection. *Journal of Personality and Social Psychology, 98*(5), 809.

Ball, D. L., & Cohen, D. K. (1999). Developing practice, developing practitioners. Toward a practice-based theory of professional education. In G. Sykes & L. Darling-Hammond (Eds.), *Teaching as the learning profession: Handbook of policy and practice* (pp. 3–33). San Francisco: Jossey-Bass.

Byrnes, K. (2012). A portrait of contemplative teaching: Embracing wholeness. *Journal of Transformative Education, 10*(1), 22–41.

Calderhead, J. (1989). Reflective teaching and teacher education. *Teaching and Teacher Education, 5*(1), 43–51.

Condon, P., Desbordes, G., Miller, W. B., & DeSteno, D. (2013). Meditation increases compassionate responses to suffering. *Psychological Science* (August), 1–3. doi:10.1177/0956797613485603.

Dahl, C. J., Lutz, A., & Davidson, R. J. (2015). Reconstructing and deconstructing the self: Cognitive mechanisms in meditation practice. *Trends in Cognitive Sciences, 19*(9), 515–523.

Davidson, R. J., & Kaszniak, A. W. (2015). Conceptual and methodological issues in research on mindfulness and meditation. *American Psychologist, 70*(7), 581.

Dewey, J. (1933). *How we think: A restatement of the relation of reflective thinking to the educative process.* Boston: D.C. Health.

Fairbanks, C. M., Duffy, G. G., Faircloth, B. S., He, Y., Levin, B., Rohr, J., & Stein, C. (2009). Beyond knowledge: Exploring why some teachers are more thoughtfully adaptive than others. *Journal of Teacher Education, 61*(1–2), 161–171.

Feiman-Nemser, S. (2012). Teacher preparation: Structural and conceptual alternatives. In *Teachers as learners* (pp. 55–104). Cambridge, MA: Harvard Education Press.

Flook, L., Goldberg, S. B., Pinger, L., Bonus, K., & Davidson, R. J. (2013). Mindfulness for teachers: A pilot study to assess effects on stress, burnout, and teaching efficacy. *Mind, Brain, and Education, 7*(3), 182–195.

Freese, A. R. (1999). The role of reflection on preservice teachers' development in the context of a professional development school. *Teaching and Teacher Education, 15*(8), 895–909.

Goyal, M., Singh, S., Sibinga, E. M. S., Gould, N. F., Rowland-Seymour, A., Sharma, R., & Haythornthwaite, J. A. (2014). Meditation programs for psychological stress and well-being: A systematic review and meta-analysis. *JAMA Internal Medicine, 174*(3), 357–368.

Hargreaves, A. (1998). The emotional practice of teaching. *Teaching and Teacher Education, 14*(8), 835–854.

Hatton, N., & Smith, D. (1995). Reflection in teacher education: Towards definition and implementation. *Teaching and Teacher Education, 11*(1), 33–49.

Howes, C., Hamilton, C. E., & Matheson, C. C. (1994). Children's relationships with peers: Differential associations with aspects of the teacher-child relationship. *Child Development, 65*(1), 253–263.

Ingersoll, R., & Merrill, L. (2012). Seven trends: The transformation of the teaching force. University of Pennsylvania, GSE Publications. Retrieved from http://repository.upenn.edu/cgi/viewcontent.cgi?article=1261&context=gse_pubs.

Jennings, P. A., & Greenberg, M. T. (2009). The prosocial classroom: Teacher social and emotional competence in relation to student and classroom outcomes. *Review of Educational Research, 79*(1), 491–525.

Kabat-Zinn, J. (1982). An outpatient program in behavioral medicine for chronic pain patients based on the practice of mindfulness meditation: Theoretical considerations and preliminary results. *General Hospital Psychiatry, 4*, 33–47.

Kabat-Zinn, J. (2003). Mindfulness-based interventions in context: Past, present, and future. *Clinical Psychology: Science and Practice, 10*(2), 144–156.

Kitchen, J. (2005). Conveying respect and empathy: Becoming a relational teacher educator. *Studying Teacher Education: A Journal of Self-Study of Teacher Education Practices, 1*(2), 195–207.

Lo, C. S. L., Ho, S. M. Y., & Hollon, S. D. (2010). The effects of rumination and depressive symptoms on the prediction of negative attributional style among college students. *Cognitive Therapy and Research, 34*, 116–123.

Loughran, J. J. (1995). *Windows into the thinking of an experienced teacher.* A paper presented at the annual meeting of the American Educational Research Association (AERA), San Francisco.

Maslach, C., Schaufeli, W. B., & Leiter, M. P. (2001). Job burnout. *Annual Review of Psychology, 52*(1), 397–422.

Muraven, M., & Baumeister, R. F. (2000). Self-regulation and depletion of limited resources: Does self-control resemble a muscle? *Psychological Bulletin, 126*(2), 247.

Nolen-Hoeksema, S. (2000). The role of rumination in depressive disorders and mixed anxiety/depressive symptoms. *Journal of Abnormal Psychology, 109*(3), 504.

Osher, D., Sprague, J., Weissberg, R. P., Axelrod, J., Keenan, S., Kendziora, K., & Zins, J. E. (2008). A comprehensive approach to promoting social, emotional, and academic growth in contemporary schools. In A. Thomas & J. Grimes (Eds.), *Best practices in school psychology V*, Vol. 4 (pp. 1263–1278). Bethesda, MD: National Association of School Psychologists.

Roeser, R. W., Schonert-Reichl, K. A., Jha, A., Cullen, M., Wallace, L., Wilensky, R., Oberle, E., Thomson, K., Taylor, C., & Harrison, J. (2013). Mindfulness training and reductions in teacher stress and burnout: Results from two randomized, waitlist-control field trials. *Journal of Educational Psychology, 105*(3), 787–804. http://doi.org/10.1037/a0032093.

Rozelle, J. J., & Wilson, S. M. (2012). Opening the black box of field experiences: How cooperating teachers' beliefs and practices shape student teachers' beliefs and practices. *Teaching and Teacher Education, 28*(8), 1196–1205.

Spilt, J. L., Hughes, J. N., Wu, J.-Y., & Kwok, O.-M. (2012). Dynamics of teacher-student relationships: Stability and change across elementary school and the influence on children's academic success. *Child Development, 83*, 1180–1195.

Tremmel, R. (1993). Zen and the art of reflective practice in teacher education. *Harvard Educational Review, 63*(4), 434–459.

Vago, D. R., & Silbersweig, D. A. (2012). Self-awareness, self-regulation, and self-transcendence (S-ART): A framework for understanding the neurobiological mechanisms of mindfulness. *Frontiers in Human Neuroscience, 6*, 296.

Wang, M. T., Brinkworth, M. E., & Eccles, J. S. (2013). The moderation effect of teacher-student relationship on the association between adolescents' self-regulation ability, family conflict, and developmental problems. *Developmental Psychology, 49*, 690–705.

Zeichner, K. M., & Liston, D. P. (2013). *Reflective teaching: An introduction.* New York: Routledge.

Chapter Four

Preparing Teachers for the Classroom

Mindful Awareness Practice in Preservice Education Curriculum

Shelley Murphy, Ontario Institute for Studies in Education/University of Toronto, Toronto, Ontario, Canada

To educate is to guide students on an inner journey towards more truthful ways of seeing and being in the world. How can schools perform their mission without encouraging the guides to scout out that inner terrain? (Palmer, 1998, p. 6)

Within Ontario, Canada, where the Ontario Institute for Studies in Education at the University of Toronto is situated, the Ministry of Education has recently published a renewed vision for classrooms that recognizes the fundamental importance of K–12 student well-being. Developing student well-being is described as supporting the whole child—academic achievement as well as cognitive, emotional, social, and physical well-being (Ontario Ministry of Education, 2014). Very few preservice teacher educator programs across Canada include a focus on supporting the social emotional learning of K–12 students or on helping preservice teachers cultivate their own capacities in this area (Schonert-Reichl & Zakrzewski, 2014).

This is problematic given that children who experience a greater sense of well-being have a greater likelihood for more positive social, emotional, and behavioral development throughout life (Awartani, Whitman, & Gordon, 2008). Furthermore, when preservice teachers have an overall sense of well-being themselves, they are more likely to have a positive impact on students' well-being and learning (Flook et al., 2013; Jennings, 2011; Meiklejohn et al., 2012).

Parker Palmer (1998) asked, "how we can expect teachers to support the inner lives of their students if they have not been supported to explore that inner terrain, themselves?" (p. 6). Holding space for teachers to explore mindfulness is a way to support both their students' and their own inner terrains. Mindfulness practices support emotional awareness and regulation. By incorporating a contemplative practice such as mindfulness within courses, preservice teachers have the opportunity to be supported through the rigorous demands of their program and to be offered tools to equally support the social, emotional, and cognitive demands of future teaching.

Within a two-year research-based Master of Teaching (MT) program that combines a graduate degree with teacher certification, a few student cohorts are introduced to mindfulness practices within their core coursework. These courses are Introduction to Special Education and Curriculum and Teaching in Literacy. Within these classes, teacher candidates learn theory and practices relevant to special education, reading, writing, and twenty-first-century literacies, inclusive education, social justice, equity, and diversity.

An equally fundamental aspect of each of these courses is a focus on promoting the resilience and social and emotional well-being of K–12 students. Preservice teacher resilience and well-being is also included as part of that focus. For this reason, mindfulness practices are incorporated into the course curriculum.

This chapter reports on a study that investigated former preservice teachers' experiences of being introduced to mindfulness practices within their preservice education program. It outlines their attitudes and perceptions toward learning about mindfulness practices within the core curriculum of their program and the impact of these practices once they had graduated and were teaching in their own classrooms.

DEFINING MINDFULNESS

Mindfulness is "the awareness that emerges through paying attention on purpose, in the present moment, and nonjudgmentally to the unfolding of experience" (Kabat-Zinn, 2003). It is a practice that often has its roots traced back to meditational practices found in Buddhism. In a Western context, it is increasingly being taught and practiced within the secular context of schooling. This may be due to increasingly convincing data showing that regular mindfulness practice helps reduce stress and anxiety (Jha, Krompinger, & Baimer, 2007; Meiklejohn et al., 2012; Roeser et al., 2013).

Mindfulness is particularly important in the field of education where studies have repeatedly that found teaching is characterized by high levels of burnout and emotional exhaustion (Dorman, 2003; Hakanen, Bakker, & Schaufeli, 2006). In fact, teachers experiencing high levels of stress for extended periods of time can develop burnout characteristics including less empathy toward students, a diminished capacity to engage and effectively teach students, and an overall lack of commitment to the teaching profession (Darr & Johns, 2008; Dorman, 2003; Roeser et al., 2012).

Although high rates of teacher stress and burnout have been well documented, research addressing potential solutions for teacher work-related stress and burnout is sparse (Meiklejohn et al., 2012; Poulin et al., 2008). There is an evident need for innovative, cost-effective ways for school systems to better support the resilience of their teachers. Perhaps this is why mindfulness-based practices are growing in popularity within the field of education. Mindfulness as one aspect of a contemplative practice has been found to reduce stress and fear while also cultivating more balance, wellness, and serenity (Schonert-Reichl & Lawlor, 2010).

Preliminary studies focused on mindfulness training for teachers have shown promising results. Recently, Flook and colleagues (2013) conducted a small pilot study to test the impact of mindfulness training for teachers. The study found that those who completed the training showed decreases in anxicty, depression, and burnout. In comparison, a group of teachers placed on a wait list for the training had increased levels of stress and burnout (Flook et al., 2013).

The same study conducted by Flook and colleagues (2013) looked at the participants' classroom performance related to behavior management and instruction. Results suggest that training in mindfulness practice resulted in improvements in observer-rated classroom organization and performance on a computer task of affective attentional bias, and increases in compassion in participants. Studies in New Zealand (Bernay, 2014), Australia (Kostanksi, 2007), and Canada (Poulin et al., 2008) showed a reduction in levels of stress for preservice teachers when they are introduced to mindfulness practices.

Given the positive effects of training in mindfulness practice for teachers, applications in teacher education programs appear promising. However, the bulk of emerging research on mindfulness for educators has been focused on in-service teacher training. There is little research conducted that details outcomes for teachers who learned about and participated in mindfulness awareness practices within a core aspect of their preservice programs. Further, there is little understanding about the most effective ways to introduce teacher candidates to mindfulness practices within their programs. The study reported on within this chapter sought to fill these gaps.

RESEARCH DESIGN, METHODOLOGY, AND DATA SOURCES

This chapter reports on one aspect of a larger study that surveyed 103 former preservice teachers who were surveyed about their experiences of learning about and participating in mindfulness practice within their program. A staggering ninety participants reported experiencing *some* initial feelings of skepticism or resistance to mindfulness practice but an eventual positive change in their response to it. Fifteen participants who reported a *significant* change in their response to mindfulness practices were randomly selected for individual interviews. These participants were interviewed to find out why their responses changed and what the outcomes were. Findings from these fifteen interviews are reported on in this chapter.

Qualitative methods of data gathering were employed in order to gather a rich and detailed understanding of the fifteen participants' opinions and experiences related to mindfulness practice. Data were gathered in the form of one thirty-minute face-to-face or Skype interview with each participant.

The interview sessions were largely open-ended, and the data was analyzed using a constant comparative method (Charmaz, 2005; Merriam, 2009; Punch, 2009). The transcribed data was read several times, segmented into meaningful analytical units, annotated, and manually coded according to repeated patterns of meaning. Transcripts were returned to the participants in order for them to perform member checks to establish credibility, reliability, and conformability (Lincoln & Guba, 1985).

Topics and practices related to mindfulness were incorporated into an overall curriculum of a special education course. Students attended twelve three-hour classes for a total of thirty-six hours. Approximately thirty minutes of each class were focused on the topic of mindfulness for a total of six hours across all class sessions. The allocated thirty minutes per class were divided into approximately three equal segments comprising a short lecture, mindfulness practice, and discussion, which are described below.

Short Lecture

Typically, lessons began with a ten-minute lecture on an aspect related to mindfulness in education such as cultivating attention and awareness, teacher/student resilience and well-being, social emotional learning, brain-based research, physiology, teaching models, and so on.

Mindfulness Practice

Next, teacher candidates were invited to participate in a ten-minute mindfulness practice such as the following:

- *mindful breathing:* focusing on the sensation of the breath;
- *mindful eating:* touching, smelling, and eating a raisin or piece of chocolate deliberately and mindfully;
- *mindful body scan:* bringing awareness to each part of the body from head to toe;
- *mindful listening:* listening mindfully to a partner speaking for five minutes;
- *mindfulness of sound:* listening to the naturally occurring sounds in and around the environment of the classroom (a ticking clock, people speaking in the hallways, cars honking on the streets, bodies shuffling, etc.);
- *mindful movement:* walking while being mindful about each step they take or to mirror the slow and deliberate actions of a partner;
- *loving-kindness meditation*: a goodwill exercise of wishing wellness, happiness, peace, and safety to themselves and others.

Students were invited to commit to at least one of these mindfulness practices at home each day for the duration of the course. They were also encouraged to incorporate mindful or deliberate awareness within the routine activities of their daily lives (e.g., while eating, washing the dishes, showering, walking, listening to someone speak, etc.). Each of these practices were discussed and modeled, where appropriate, within the class.

Discussion

After the lecture and mindfulness practices, approximately ten minutes were spent discussing teacher candidates' experiences, challenges, barriers, and questions related to their personal mindfulness practices. Although students were neither asked to nor required to incorporate mindfulness practice within their student teaching practicum placements, many of them freely chose to do so. Within this discussion period, students took the opportunity to share details about these experiences (e.g., practical applications, successes, challenges, barriers, etc.).

FINDINGS

Initial Resistance

Each of the fifteen graduates interviewed reported experiencing feelings of skepticism or resistance to mindfulness practice at the start of the course before changing to a more positive response. For example, when Andrea heard the term mindfulness, she said, "I thought, 'oh, this is so hippie dippy,' it reminded me of yoga which I don't love. So, I kind of wrote it off it first."

Sharon, who had never heard of mindfulness practice before the class, described her reaction as "curious but very skeptical." As she explained: "it's hard to believe now, but when you first mentioned it to our class I honestly thought it was going to be kind of hokey. I had no idea how much it would impact me and my teaching." Similarly, other participants used terms such as "lame," "irrelevant," "awkward," and "waste of time" to describe their initial responses.

Two former teacher candidates reported having strong feelings of resistance due, in part, to their religious understandings. As Becky commented, "I was hesitant initially because I grew up Christian and my mother was always telling me to be careful of the bells and to be careful about clearing my mind. I thought that's what it was going to be."

Similarly, Rubia described learning about the danger of *clearing the mind* in Sunday school. She said, "I was taught keeping the mind idle or clearing it opens room for the devil to come in. I thought mindfulness was supposed to help you clear your mind so I wasn't really so open to it." Both Rubia and Becky's concerns were soon eased when they learned that mindfulness practice was not an exercise of clearing the mind but of bringing awareness to the present moment.

Andrew attributed his initial resistance to an aversion to focusing his attention on his breath. He felt very uncomfortable with the idea of focusing on his breath because it was a trigger for his anxiety. He said,

> At first when you said most of us would be using our breath as an anchor I thought, "I can't, it will give me a panic attack" but as soon as you said we had the option of finding another "anchor" I became more open to it. So, for me, it helps to use a visual image or to focus on my every day, as you said, like washing the dishes or walking or whatever.

Although each of the fifteen graduates interviewed experienced an initial resistance to the idea of learning about and practicing mindfulness within the course, they came to view it as valuable. In particular, they reported better management of their levels of stress, a positive impact on their teaching once in the field, and a positive ripple effect on the lives of friends, family members, colleagues, and students.

Better Management of Stress

Over time, mindfulness practice helped the majority of the fifteen interviewees manage their feelings of stress and anxiety while in their preservice program and beyond. Fourteen of the fifteen graduates felt mindfulness practice had become a *primary* tool for mediating their levels of stress. As Julia, a recent graduate from the program, said, "This past year was the first academic year that I wasn't hospitalized because of my Crohn's disease and I know it's because mindfulness helped me to manage my stress." Similarly, Becky explained,

> My classmates and I really looked forward to your class because we knew you would be doing mindfulness with us and so many of us were so overwhelmed. I'm usually a very busy person and I can't sit down. Literally things are always fire-working in my mind and doing the breathing was amazing. I can actually refocus whereas before I would just get completely overwhelmed. It was huge, personally, for me.

For Sharon, who had been teaching third grade for three years since graduating, practicing mindfulness helped her to cope with feeling overwhelmed. She said,

> It was a big deal to learn how to notice when we're starting to go into the stress response and have a way to actually stop it. I couldn't believe the stress reducing, calming benefits it had on me during stressful times as a student so I never stopped. It's having a significant impact on me now as a teacher.

Positive Impact on Teaching

All of the preservice graduates within the study voluntarily incorporated mindfulness practices within their practicum classrooms while they were still in the program. At the time of the study, fourteen of the fifteen of them were continuing to incorporate mindfulness practices into their daily teaching routines once in the field. They did so because they recognized the myriad benefits for themselves as teachers and for their students.

Raj, who at the time of the study incorporated mindfulness practices within his seventh grade classroom and voluntarily led a Mindfulness Club for the school community, explained, "It's amazing—behavior management is better and students have shared how they have personally started using breathing exercises and such in school and in their life outside of school when they are feeling stressed." Andrew also spoke of the way mindfulness practice has supported him and his teaching. He said,

> I'm an anxious person anyway but being new to the profession there is a lot of pressure. I start my own day with a mindfulness practice and then we do it in class. I think it's helped me create mindful spaces for my students and I'm much less stressed and reactive. That's saying a lot for me because I have thirty-five students and it can get very overwhelming.

Nada's comment was representative of many of the participants' thoughts. She explained, "For me, mindfulness is a one stop shop. It's classroom management, it's helping them with mental health, with their attention and it helps me deal with how stressful it is to be a new teacher. It's all of it." At the time of the study, Nada continued to participate in daily mindful breathing practices at home while also inviting her students to participate in daily mindfulness practices within the classroom.

Ripple Effect

Many former teacher candidates referred to a *ripple type effect* that resulted from learning about mindfulness. Once they came to notice the benefits of engaging in mindfulness practices for themselves, many of them introduced it to their friends and family members, as well as within their practicum placements, to their supervising teacher, colleagues, and students. For example, Andrea, Julia, and Joey spoke about the continued positive impact mindfulness practice was having on their loved ones.

Andrea, who introduced it to her husband, explained, "we live in a tiny space and we stop and focus on our breathing together every night. It's helped our relationship." Joey, who was the only participant who did not continue with mindfulness once he graduated, said learning about mindfulness continues to affect him positively in an indirect way. Though he felt mindfulness did not match his personality for the "long run," he introduced it to his girlfriend who continues to practice it regularly to support stress management in her work as a social worker.

Each of the former candidates voluntarily incorporated mindfulness practices within at least one of their practicum placements while in their teacher education program. For Christine, incorporating these practices influenced her supervising teachers within two of her placements. She said, "Both of my supervising teachers last year continued with the practice after I left. Learning about this has had a ripple effect out there." Similarly, Rubia said:

> I would see kids pointing to their brains talking about using their breath to make wiser choices. It was really something. By the end of practicum, other teachers were coming in to ask us about what was happening in our class. Students seemed a little calmer and more respectful toward each other. The other teachers started to notice. The same thing is happening here [present teaching context] and I'm teaching them.

FACTORS CONTRIBUTING TO CHANGE

Three key factors influenced how teacher candidates experienced mindfulness practice within their teacher education program. For many, these factors contributed to a change from an initial negative opinion to a more positive response and a commitment to practice. The *first* was that mindfulness approaches were taught as part of the curriculum for at least one of their required courses on a weekly basis. Andrea's comment represents the responses of many. She said, "If it hadn't been for our class, I'm sure I never would've looked into it."

The *second* factor was the manner in which mindfulness was introduced. While students were expected to participate in lectures and discussions on the topic of mindfulness in education, they were not required to participate in a practice. As Melanie said, "It wasn't pushed on us—that was important. It freed me up to come to it in my own time."

The graduates also appreciated learning about current research related to mindfulness practice and its impact on brain function, physiology, executive functioning, resiliency, and so on. This appeared to help legitimize mindfulness practice for them. The *third* factor was the observable impact on their personal and professional lives and the ripple effect.

On noticing the positive outcomes of mindfulness practice for themselves, for their family members and loved ones, and for their students within their practicum placements, preservice teachers became further convinced of the benefits of mindfulness practice. This deepened their commitment to continued practice within their personal lives and their future teaching. As Elizabeth said,

> I'm grateful to have been introduced to mindfulness in the [program] because it's changed so much in me. It also gave me the courage to bring it into the classroom and now it's a school wide initiative. We have a mindful minute at the beginning of every day over the PA system and it's all because I learned about it in class.

CONCLUSION

While each of the graduates interviewed for this study experienced feelings of skepticism or resistance to mindfulness practice at the start of the course, they reported a significant positive change in their opinions and responses to it. Overall, they experienced improvements in their ability to manage their levels of stress, a positive impact on their teaching in the classroom, and noticeable benefits for their students and for others who had the opportunity to learn about mindfulness from them.

Three key factors contributed to the graduates' positive experiences. First, mindfulness was taught as part of the core curriculum of a required course over an extended period of time. Second, they were invited rather than required to participate in mindfulness practices. Third, they noticed the benefits and positive outcomes for themselves and for their students, friends, and loved ones who participated as well. This catalyzed their further interest in mindfulness practice.

The findings from this study add to the growing body of knowledge that suggests that mindfulness is a potentially valuable component of preservice education programs. Although mindfulness techniques are rarely included within teacher education programs, when they are, they are often offered as elective courses or as additional workshops. These often come at considerable cost and time commitment for preservice teacher candidates and may reduce the likelihood that teacher candidates who are not familiar with mindfulness or who have negative notions about it will participate.

Including mindfulness practices within preservice curriculum can serve as a unique entry point for introducing and integrating contemplative practices to support the well-being and success of individuals who are teacher candidates and eventually practicing teachers. As such, it also has the potential to support the well-being and success of their students in the classroom.

ESSENTIAL IDEAS TO CONSIDER

- Applications of mindfulness practices in teacher education programs appear promising.
- Teacher candidates are more likely to respond positively to mindfulness practices when they are incorporated into their teacher education classes on a regular basis and when they are invited rather than required to participate.
- When teacher candidates show initial resistance to mindfulness practices, this can often give way to a more positive response over time.
- Regular mindfulness practices have the potential to help teacher candidates manage their feelings of stress and anxiety while in their preservice program and once teaching in the field.

REFERENCES

Awartani, M., Whitman, C., & Gordon, J. (2008). Developing instruments to capture young people's perceptions of how school as a learning environment affects their well-being. *European Journal of Education, 43*, 51–71.

Bernay, R. S. (2014). Mindfulness and the beginning teacher. *Australian Journal of Teacher Education, 39*(7). http://dx.doi.org/10.14221/ajte.2014v39n7.6.

Charmaz, K. (2005). Grounded theory in the 21st century: A qualitative method for advancing social justice research. In N. K. Denzin & Y. Lincoln (Eds.), *Handbook of qualitative research* (3rd ed.). Thousand Oaks, CA: Sage.

Darr, W., & Johns, G. (2008). Work strain, health and absenteeism: A meta-analysis. *Journal of Occupational Health Psychology, 13*(4), 293–318. doi:10.1037/a0012639.

Dorman, J. (2003). Testing a model for teacher burnout. *Australian Journal of Educational & Developmental Psychology, 3*, 35–47.

Flook, L., Goldberg, S. B., Pinger, L., Bonus, K., & Davidson, R. J. (2013). Mindfulness for teachers: A pilot study to assess effects on stress, burnout, and teaching efficacy. *Mind, Brain, and Education, 7*(3), 182–195.

Lincoln, Y. S., & Guba, E. G. (1985). *Naturalistic inquiry.* Newbury Park, CA: Sage Publications.

Hakanen, J., Bakker, A., & Schaufeli, W. (2006). Burnout and working engagement among teachers. *Journal of School Psychology, 4*, 495–513.

Jennings, P. A. (2011). Promoting teachers' social and emotional competencies to support performance and reduce burnout. In A. Cohan and A. Honigsfeld (Eds.), *Breaking the mold of pre-service and in-service teacher education: Innovative and successful practices for the 21st century.* Lanham, MD: Rowman & Littlefield Education.

Jha, A., Krompinger, J, & Baimer, M. (2007). Mindfulness training modifies subsystems of attention. *Cognitive, Affective, and Behavioral Neuroscience, 7*(2), 109–119. doi:10.3758/cabn.7.2.109. http://dx.doi.org/10.3758/CABN.7.2.109.

Kabat-Zinn, J. (2003). Mindfulness-based interventions in context: Past, present, and future. *Clinical Psychology: Science and Practice, 10*(2), 144–156.

Kostanski, M. (2007). The role of mindfulness in reducing stress for pre-service students. Paper presented at the Australian Association for Research and Education conference.

Meiklejohn, J., Phillips, C., Freedman, M. L., Griffin, M. L., Biegel, G., Roach, A., Frank, J., Burke, C., Pinger, L., Soloway, G., Isberg, R., Sibinga, E., Grossman, L., & Saltzman, A. (2012). Integrating mindfulness training into K–12 education: Fostering the resilience of teachers and students. *Mindfulness, 3*(4), 291–307.

Merriam, S. (2009). *Qualitative research: A guide to design and implementation.* San Francisco: Jossey-Bass.

Ontario Ministry of Education. (2014). *Achieving excellence: A renewed vision for education in Ontario.* Toronto, Ontario, Canada: Queen's Printer for Ontario.

Palmer, P. (1998). *The courage to teach: Exploring the inner landscape of a teacher's life.* San Francisco: Jossey-Bass.

Poulin, P. A., Mackenzie, C. S., Soloway, G., & Karayolas, E. (2008). Mindfulness training as an evidenced-based approach to reducing stress and promoting well-being among human services professionals. *International Journal of Health Promotion and Education, 46*, 35–43.

Punch, F. (2009). *Introduction to research methods in education.* London: Sage.

Roeser, R. W., Schonert-Reichl, K. A., Jha, A., Cullen, M., Wallace, L., Wilensky, R., Oberle, E., Thomson, K., Taylor, C., & Harrison, J. (2013). Mindfulness training and reductions in teacher stress and burnout: Results from two randomized, waitlist-control field trials. *Journal of Educational Psychology, 105*(3), 787–804.

Roeser, R. W., Skinner, E., Beers, J., & Jennings, P. A. (2012). Mindfulness training and teachers' professional development: An emerging area of research and practice. *Child Development Perspectives, 6*, 167–173. doi:10.1111/j.1750-8606.2012.00238.x.

Schonert-Reichl, K. A., & Lawlor, M. S. (2010). The effects of a mindfulness-based education program on pre- and early adolescents' well-being and social and emotional competence. *Mindfulness, 1*(3), 137–151.

Schonert-Reichl, K., & Zakrzewski, V. (2014). How to close the social-emotional gap in teacher training. *Greater Good.* Retrieved from https://greatergood.berkeley.edu/article/item/how_to_close_the_social_emotional_gap_in_teacher_training.

Chapter Five

Contemplative Teacher Education, Teacher Identity, and Relationship-Building Strategies

Anne Maj Nielsen and Per F. Laursen,
Aarhus University, Copenhagen, Denmark

Students' relationships with their teachers and classmates are important for their learning and well-being, and there is currently growing scholarly interest in the contribution that schools can make to promote students' mental health and emotional competence (Weare, 2004). Teachers are increasingly expected to develop their students' social and emotional competence as well as life and communication skills, which are regarded as some of the most important skills in the twenty-first century (Bellanca & Brandt, 2010; Goleman & Senge, 2014).

However, the setting in which teachers are expected to develop these skills is becoming increasingly challenging. The number of students perceived as disruptive in the classroom has increased over recent years and, in many countries, special needs students are now included in mainstream classrooms (Jennings, 2011). Teachers are thus expected to meet increasingly stringent demands in conditions with increasing perceived disruptions and difficult interactions with students in class.

These conditions call for relational competence. A recent systematic review of research on teacher competences found relational competence to be equally as important as subject competence and classroom management competence (Nordenbo et al., 2008).

Relational competence is the teacher's professional competence to overcome difficult interactions and to build supportive relationships with students. According to Juul & Jensen (2002), the relationally competent teacher has the ability to:

> "see" the individual child on the child's own terms and to adapt his or her own behavior accordingly without thereby relinquishing the leadership responsibility, as well as the ability to remain authentic in the contact with the child and the ability and willingness to take full responsibility for the quality of the relationship. (p. 128)

It is this definition of relational competence that we will employ throughout this chapter.

In this chapter, we present the results of a study that we conducted on a program in relational competence that was taught in a university college in Denmark as part of a Danish teacher education program. We will begin by outlining this program in relational competence and its place within the wider Danish teacher education program. We will then describe the theoretical framework on which our study of the relational competence program was based, and, finally, we will present the results of the study and their practical significance for teacher education.

TEACHER EDUCATION IN DENMARK AND THE PROGRAM IN RELATIONAL COMPETENCE

Teacher education in Denmark lasts four years; it comprises a theoretical curriculum and one to two teaching placements every year. In the theoretical part of the program, the preservice teachers learn school subjects, didactics, and some learning psychology and, in the teaching placements, the preservice teachers observe and learn from experienced teachers. The further they proceed through the program, the more the preservice teachers are expected to teach on their own and "learn by doing."

The study described in this chapter followed a project at a university college in Denmark in which two classes within the teacher education program were adapted to include contemplative teaching in relational competence. This contemplative teaching was conducted throughout the entire four years of the program—from 2012 to 2016—and included fifty preservice teachers in total. This chapter presents and analyzes the results of the first two years of the project.

During the first two years of the project, the preservice teachers participated in a full-day seminar every month that included theoretical discussions on pedagogy in addition to contemplative training. The seminar began with a short welcome and a communal physical activity, such as a guided, simple dance, followed by the presentation and discussion of a particular theory—for example, a theory about how children require relational patterns based on mentalization and the development of self in interactions with parents (Fona-gy et al., 2005; Stern, 1998), or how adults who are aware of their own response patterns and can adopt the child's perspective can also change inter-actions and give the child new relationship opportunities (see Jensen, Skib-sted, & Christensen, 2015).

During the seminar, preservice teachers took part in guided mindfulness meditations that focused on breath and/or the body. Seminars also included guided activities with relational contact, such as massage, where preservice teachers gave each other gentle neck and shoulder massages while being prompted to be mindfully aware of sensations and experiences in the situa-tion.

After this guided activity, they were invited to reflect on their personal experiences and to connect these experiences to situations in which they had experienced difficult relationships—either in school or another context. These reflections were shared in groups and reflected on collectively using the previously presented theory to understand their own as well as others' experiences.

This contemplative preservice teacher education also included project-specific concepts. The phrase "60 percent at home—40 percent in the other" was a project-specific concept used to express the importance of remember-ing to be mindfully aware of oneself (60 percent) with integrity in order to be mindfully aware of the other (40 percent) in a relation. The 60/40 percent framing was used to help the preservice teachers remember to be mindfully aware of themselves and to accept thoughts and feelings in order to cope with the situation and control their emotions.

Preservice teachers were also encouraged to consider various examples from more experienced teachers' classroom management and relationship-building practices. These teachers would usually present a case about a stu-dent having difficulty at school and how they attempted—often successful-ly—to relate competently in order to support the student, often reflecting on what they could have done differently.

The contemplative training therefore comprised knowledge about rela-tional psychology; this training took place individually, in pairs, and in groups.

The program in contemplative teaching and relational competence was delivered by a psychologist and an educator with many years of experience with meditation and relational processes. Some of the teacher educators and supervisors also attended contemplative teaching courses and included se-lected exercises in their teaching of other subject lessons with the project classes.

Wherever possible, the preservice teachers in the project had their teach-ing placement training with teachers who had been engaged in contemplative teaching and mindful awareness of relationship building with students. This allowed the preservice teachers to learn by observation and to be supported and supervised in practice when needed.

THEORY: HOW CAN CONTEMPLATIVE EDUCATION CONTRIBUTE TO RELATIONAL COMPETENCE?

The fact that contemplative practices helped the preservice teachers become aware of their emotions and cognitive practices can provide an insight into the learning outcomes of contemplative education. The body-phenomenology approach provides a coherent theoretical framework to conceptualize and study sensory experiences, emotions, and thoughts (Merleau-Ponty, 1945/2014; Petitmengin & Bitbol, 2009). On a body-phenomenological approach, the preservice teachers' attempts to establish and maintain a supportive relationship with students in class are conceptualized as an intentional attitude toward the students.

With this approach, a person is always intentionally oriented from their first-person perspective toward the world, and phenomena in the world simultaneously appeal for the person's attention and intention (Merleau-Ponty, 1945/2014). On the body-phenomenological approach, attention is essentially responsive: when something happens, the person responds to the change by becoming attentive to the new situation (Waldenfels, 2011). In teacher education, the preservice teachers learn to respond with attention to the meaningful learning outcomes.

During a teaching placement, however, students in class can behave in ways that cause the preservice teacher to respond with attention to phenomena that are irrelevant to the meaningful learning outcomes. Such a phenomenon could be the preservice teacher's own emotions—for example, anger or helplessness in response to a disruptive student. It is possible that such an emotional response played a role in a similar situation during the preservice teacher's childhood or adolescence, and that this kind of attentional response has therefore formed the basis of their experience-based, immediate interpretation of the situation (Stern, 1998, 2004).

When such emotional reactions occupy the preservice teacher's field of attention, they are at risk of reacting emotionally and may be unable to act as a relationally competent professional.

On the body-phenomenological approach, however, preservice teachers are not only responsive but intentionally orient themselves toward what is meaningful in the world. The preservice teacher can (learn to) intentionally maintain focus on a specific activity even if something else appeals for their attention (Leontiev, 1994). For example, if a class reading activity is disturbed by noisy students, the teacher can learn to remain calm, identify the cause of the noise, and guide the noisy students toward a nondisruptive way to participate (instead of responding to the noise as a threat and displaying anger).

The preservice teacher can learn to remain calm by not immediately interpreting the situation, for example, by employing emotional attention. Preservice teachers can attempt to become aware of their own patterns of response—the impulse to feel affected, interpret, and react in specific ways—without acting on them. They can attempt to be open to and contemplate the experience and the phenomena, which could involve their relationship to a child or class. Practice and training is important in order to approach other people with an open attitude, and it is necessary that preservice teachers maintain an open and reflexive attitude toward themselves as well as others.

In the contemplative training project, mindfulness meditation included embodied training of relational attention, which helped preservice teachers develop an awareness of both their own and the other's perspective. Training one's attitude and one's ability to change perspective can arguably create an empathetic and understanding approach to other people as well as to oneself: "A teacher with a contemplative orientation attempts to teach with compassion, integrity, and mindful awareness" (Byrnes, 2012, p. 24).

RESEARCH METHODS

In our study of preservice teachers' experiences in the relational competence program, their degree course, and their school practice, the phenomenological approach and theory formed the basis for methodology and method (Petitmengin & Bitbol, 2009). In order to study the preservice teachers' experiences, we conducted qualitative in-depth interviews in which we asked for detailed descriptions of significant incidents in their placement training. Interviews were conducted with groups of three to five preservice teachers, which enabled the preservice teachers to describe their specific experiences individually before reflecting on them collectively. The method and interview questions are described in more detail below.

RESEARCH DESIGN AND PARTICIPANTS

Two classes were randomly selected by the university college to participate in the project. In total, fifty preservice teachers participated—slightly more female than male—all of whom participated from the beginning of their teacher education program.

The majority of the participants were ethnic Danes in their twenties. Fewer than ten participants had other ethnic backgrounds. Twelve preservice teachers from the project classes (the "project group") were interviewed in the late spring of 2014, shortly after they had completed their preservice training and were halfway through their four-year teacher education program. Ten preservice teachers from a control group (who had received no contemplative training) were also interviewed. All twenty-two interviewees volunteered.

In order to recall lived experiences the preservice teachers regarded as significant during their recent placement, the interviews were preceded by a body-scan meditation, after which the preservice teachers were invited to recall an incident involving positive contact with a student ("a good relation") and an incident in which they felt they had been a good teacher ("teacher identity"). After guidance, the students had ten minutes to draw the incident.

When each preservice teacher had presented their drawing and described the incident and its significance to the group, the focus group discussed the individual and common features of their experiences. The interviewer asked questions that encouraged the preservice teachers to reflect on their performances in order to become mindfully aware of their experiences, relations, interactions, and teaching in the complex classroom practice in their latest teaching placement. For example, one of the groups discussed their incidents and concluded that it was important to be present in the situation:

Interviewer: Is this something you do? Or does it happen by accident? Do you know how to do it?

Preservice teacher A: Well, first of all, I always need to breathe if I feel like I can't be in the situation. And the thought that it is only a moment in which you are situated—it is not you—it is the situation you find difficult to handle. And that is something you can learn.

Interviewer: So it is good to know that—and important to breathe?

Preservice teacher B: I think it is just as important to somehow be able to recognize how you are feeling presently, like: now I am really getting nervous—that is OK. And then take it from there. To accept that now you are in that condition for a little while, and just be with it.

Our study's thematic and analytical approach followed Giorgi (2012). Each transcript was read in its entirety, important themes and breaches were cited in the text, and the themes and phenomena were rephrased by the researchers. Common themes as well as variations between the project group and the control group were defined.

RESULTS: TEACHER IDENTITY AND
RELATIONSHIP-BUILDING STRATEGIES

Many experiences and perceptions were similar in both the project and the control group, which is not surprising given that 95 percent of the teacher education content in both groups is identical. The preservice teachers' shared experiences included engaging the entire class in a subject, and their good relations with students involved helping students with difficulties to improve their academic results and self-confidence. Across the two groups, the preservice teachers considered it meaningful to have good relationships with their students and to make a difference academically and/or personally, and they found it important that they were becoming teachers whilst maintaining their identity as individuals.

The most important variations between the project group and the control group were their different experiences of becoming a teacher, taking on a teacher identity or relating to the teacher's role, and building relationships with students in challenging conditions. In the following section these variations are examined more closely.

Teacher Identity or Role

The preservice teachers in the project group regarded the teacher's role as something that can be entered into and withdrawn from. Even if someone *is* a teacher (or in the process of becoming one), it is possible to withdraw from the role and to engage in a more informal person-to-person contact with the students.

The preservice teachers' mindful awareness of themselves makes it possible to adopt a more distanced and reflective approach which can make it easier to establish close contact with students. They can experiment with the role, they can show students in class that they are both a teacher and an ordinary human being, and they can occasionally withdraw from the role of the teacher altogether in order to form a closer and more informal relationship with the students.

One preservice teacher said that this ability to enter into and withdraw from the teacher's role was developed by the relational competence program:

> I think perhaps this relational course has taught us that using this option is OK.
> In other words, that you say: I am just me, and this is what I have to offer. That
> you must be professional at all times, but that you don't always have to sit
> there looking up how you should react in the answer book.

Another preservice teacher was aware that it is never possible to completely withdraw from the teacher's role when you are in school with students, but that it is possible to distance yourself from it and indicate to the students that, although you are a teacher, you are also a person. Another preservice teacher framed it as a matter of balance:

> It [the project] has heightened my awareness of how I can enter into the teacher's role. And this largely relates to the act of striking a balance between the professional and the personal. While being true to yourself at the same time. And not compromising your own principles and values, things like that. . . . If I open up to them [the students], I feel that they usually open up to me, too. And I have had lots of positive experiences of this happening.

It is important to discern which personal experiences and values may or may not be helpful and necessary in teacher-student relationships. Likewise, it is essential to study how personal values and patterns of responsivity may develop through education.

The 60/40 "balancing frame" described above relates to one of the main points of the contemplative training program, namely that you have to be mindfully aware of yourself if you wish to get in touch with the students. Several preservice teachers in the project group embraced this point. One preservice teacher explained:

> In my opinion, I have wholeheartedly embraced this 60–40 balance—being 60 percent grounded in yourself. If I'm going to give myself, I have to be firmly grounded in myself and know exactly what I'm bringing with me and have to offer, and what I can give today, right now.

Another preservice teacher described an incident in which he sensed that the students did not understand what he was explaining. He tried different ways of explaining without success. He eventually grew impatient and was just about to "fly off the handle" but then "restrained [him]self." He used the metaphor about being 60 percent aware of himself:

> And then I thought, "Now I have to take a deep breath, and another one, and start again." I can really remember that it had a profound effect on me, the deep breathing and then trying to start again. Thinking of a different way to explain it.

The interviewed preservice teachers who participated in the relational competence program (the project group) considered it valuable to be able to withdraw from the teacher's role and say "I am who I am" and to mindfully reflect on and experiment with teaching to improve their skills and teaching competence.

In contrast, the interviewed preservice teachers who did not participate in the relational competence program (the control group) tended to think it was important to tailor a specific version of the teacher's role to one's own personality and to gradually shape one's own teaching role based on experience. One preservice teacher claimed, "I don't think I will be a good teacher until ten years from now; in other words, when I truly feel that I have everything fairly well under control."

The control group claimed that challenges and emotions were mixed in their personal-professional role. In contrast, the project group used the 60/40 percent framing to remember being mindfully aware of themselves and to accept thoughts and feelings. By changing these attentive patterns of response, they have learned to suspend the impulse to react immediately; they have also been given the opportunity to regain balance and consider fresh approaches to teaching and the teacher-student relationship.

Fortuitous and Intended Relationship Building

Preservice teachers in both the project group and the control group were aware of their relations to students as they experienced them during in-service teaching training. This is not surprising given that topics dealing with relations to students are part of the general teacher education curriculum. However, teachers in the project group and the control group presented very different examples of what they considered to be experiences of good relationship building with students.

The descriptions by preservice teachers in the control group were of situations in fortuitous circumstances in which they became aware that their friendly and welcoming attitude could make students respond with interest and thus support good relationship building. We call these instances *fortuitous relationship building* as they depended on the students' accepting response to the preservice teachers' inviting attitude. If the student did not respond in this way, the preservice teachers explained that they were reluctant to engage further in relationship building with the particular student.

In contrast, the descriptions by preservice teachers in the project group were of situations in which they consciously decided to build and/or change a relationship. In these cases, the preservice teachers expressed a reflected intention to assume an open and inviting approach regardless of how the student initially responded. They deliberately tried to change unsatisfactory relationships and their relationship building mostly revolved around interacting with students in order to support relationship building and engage the students in school activities. We call these incidents *intended relationship building*.

The following quotation is an example of fortuitous relationship building involving a preservice teacher and a female student in the third grade (nine years old) who is described as generally moody and dismissive:

> It started when I decided to contact her and notice how she reacts. I thought that if she didn't react, I'd just carry on. But then she did react . . . I tried to

> keep the conversation going by asking a lot of questions, not necessarily about
> the English lesson. . . . And I think that I managed to create a good relationship
> there in the end.

This preservice teacher invited the student into a conversation and she responded, so he engaged further with her. According to the preservice teacher, the student regularly rejected his attempts to converse with her, and, if she had done so again, he would have concentrated on the other students. However, fortunately, she responded on this occasion, leading to a development in their relationship.

The following quotation is an example of *intended relationship building* in which a preservice teacher describes his experience with a student who had difficulties in math and refused to speak to him.

> I thought to myself: "this is not right—now I must take some responsibility for
> this relationship as a teacher." The first couple of times I sat by him he didn't
> talk to me at all. He wrote in his diary, which had nothing to do with math, but
> I ignored that. When the class was doing geometry on the computer, I praised
> him, perhaps too much—but then he began to open up. In the end, we had a
> good relationship.

The preservice teacher's intentional, persistent, and compassionate approach to the student over several days eventually contributed to a relationship in which supportive academic and personal interaction became possible.

This preservice teacher assumed responsibility for relationship building even though it represented a personal challenge. He reported that contemplative teaching had equipped him with the ability to stay calm and compassionate with the student until the student trusted him.

Some of the preservice teachers who engaged in intended relationship building experienced discomfort or even panic once they had decided to change a relationship but did not know how the student would react to their invitation for contact. During interviews, these teachers were asked why they intended to build relationships with students during training even though they experienced it as emotionally challenging.

They explained that they were motivated by the psychological theories about relationship building taught in the relational competence program. They also explained how they balanced their emotions in the challenging situations with contemplative practices they had learned in the relational competence program.

Incidents of *fortuitous* and *intended relationship building* in the groups are illustrated in Table 5.1.

As can be seen in Table 5.1, in the project group, ten preservice teachers described experiences with intended relationship building, while two participants described experiences with fortuitous relationship building. In the con-

Table 5.1.

	Project Group	Control Group
Intended relationship building	10	1
Fortuitous relationship building	2	9
Total	12	10

trol group, nine preservice teachers described experiences with fortuitous relationship building, while a single participant described an experience with intended relationship building.

However, as opposed to the preservice teachers in the project group, who attributed their intentional relationship building to the skills they learned in the relational competence program, this single teacher attributed her attempt to intentionally build a relationship with a student (despite the associated challenges) to events she had experienced at home with her young daughter.

This indicates that intended relationship building can be learned in education as well as in other life experiences. The differences between the project group and the control group indicate that the relational competence project has equipped many of the preservice teachers with the skills to pursue intended relationship building. Three-quarters of those interviewed in the project group expressed intentional relationship building to be part of their future profession as a teacher.

DISCUSSION

How did contemplative teaching in the project group contribute to the preservice teachers' learning and development of relational competence?

The preservice teachers in the relational competence program learned about relationship building through theory, examples, and experiences, as they were trained in the mindful awareness of their own sensory, emotional, and cognitive patterns of response and in the mindful awareness of others. The contemplative practices provided them with opportunities to acquire a mindful awareness of their emotions and patterns of response as well as a repertoire of contemplative activities.

In practice, 75 percent of those interviewed were able to use contemplative practices to remain emotionally balanced and maintain contact with the students and leadership in class even in challenging situations.

During the relational competence program, the preservice teachers also experimented with and experienced a wide variety of relational interaction situations. In such experiments, they were guided and encouraged to be mindfully aware of their experiences and to use contemplative practices to restore balance. The meaning and value of balance and relationship-building competence was supported and explained in practice as they shared personal experiences and reflections using theories and concepts in their community of preservice teachers.

The preservice teachers in the project group differed from those in the control group as they were able to distinguish themselves from the teacher role, accept their emotions, and calm themselves with contemplative practices. These results correspond with the findings in Dorman (2015) that preservice teachers who participate in mindful and centering activities develop social-emotional competence, social awareness, and relationship skills by cultivating self-awareness and self-management through being present and self-observing.

Contemplative teaching in a secular environment has attracted growing interest among teachers and researchers, and Byrnes (2012) suggests that this is due to its emphasis on the wholeness of body and mind, emotion and intellect, and learning and teaching. Contemplative teaching begins by knowing and experiencing ourselves directly (Byrnes, 2012, p. 23).

This is not easy to combine with the "many contemporary mainstream educational practices that emphasize isolated knowledge and transmission" (Byrnes, 2012, p. 24). Such mainstream practices, which are also common in Denmark, most likely encourage teachers to approach themselves and their students instrumentally, governed by standards separate from the living processes in classroom practice.

CONCLUSION

This study suggests that the preservice teachers' personal experiences and mindful awareness training, together with their commitment to using their knowledge and experiences of relationship building, stand out as important resources for their future education and teaching careers. These resources provide them with a foundation to reason about and focus on their intended relationship-building efforts.

Future Research

In order to develop and improve the teacher education program in the future, it is important to learn more about which life experiences and practices in this program can help preservice teachers to build relationships and be mindfully aware throughout their education and teaching. It is promising that the students in our study appeared to thrive with contemplative teacher education, and this suggests that future research should study opportunities for sustainable teaching and education with contemplative education.

ESSENTIAL IDEAS TO CONSIDER

- Relational competence is an important part of teacher competence.
- Contemplative teacher education can contribute to the development of relational competence.
- Intended relationship building is an important aspect of teachers' relational competence.

ACKNOWLEDGMENTS

Our thanks to the Danish Society for the Promotion of Life Wisdom in Children, to teachers and preservice teachers at VIA University College in Aarhus, and to the placement teachers who made this project possible.

REFERENCES

Bellanca, J., & Brandt, R. (2010). *21st century skills*. Bloomington, IN: Solution Tree Press.

Byrnes, K. (2012). A portrait of contemplative teaching: Embracing wholeness. *Journal of Transformative Education, 10*(1), 22–41.

Dorman, E. H. (2015). Building teachers' social-emotional competence through mindfulness practices. *Curriculum and Teaching Dialogue, 17*(1–2), 103–119.

Fonagy, P., Gergely, G., Jurist, E. L. & Target, M. (2005). *Affect regulation, mentalization, and the development of the self*. New York: Other Press.

Giorgi, A. (2012). The descriptive phenomenological psychological method. *Journal of Phenomenological Psychology, 43*, 3–12.

Goleman, D., & Senge, P. (2014). *The triple focus. A new approach to education*. Florence, MA: More Than Sound.

Hart, T. (2004). Opening the contemplative mind in the classroom. *Journal of Transformative Education, 2*(1), 28–46.

Jennings, P. A. (2011). Promoting teachers' social and emotional competencies to support performance and reduce burnout. In A. Cohan & A. Honigsfeld (Eds.), *Breaking the mold of pre-service and in-service teacher education: Innovative and successful practices for the 21st century* (pp. 133–143). Lanham, MD: Rowman & Littlefield.

Jensen, E., Skibsted, E. B., & Christensen, M. V. (2015). Educating teachers focusing on the development of reflective and relational competences. *Educational Research for Policy and Practice, 14*(3), 201–212.

Juul, J., & Jensen, H. (2002). *Pædagogisk relationskompetence*. Copenhagen: Apostrof.

Leontiev, A. (1994). The development of voluntary attention in the child. In R. V. d. Veer & J. Valsiner (Eds.), *The Vygotsky reader* (pp. 289–312). Oxford: Blackwell Publishers.

Merleau-Ponty, M. (1945/2014). *Phenomenology of perception*. New York: Routledge.

Nordenbo, S. E., Søgaard Larsen, M., Tiftikci, N., Wendt, R. E., & Østergaard, S. (2008). *Lærerkompetencer og elevers læring i førskole og skole*. Copenhagen: Dansk Clearinghouse for Uddannelsesforskning, DPU, University of Aarhus.

Petitmengin, C. & M. Bitbol (2009). The validity of first-person descriptions as authenticity and coherence. *Journal of Consciousness Studies, 16*(10–12): 363–404.

Stern, D. N. (1998). *The interpersonal world of the infant*. London: Karnac Books.

Stern, D. N. (2004). *The present moment in psychotherapy and everyday life*. New York: W. W. Norton.

Waldenfels, B. (2011). *Phenomenology of the alien*. Evanston, IL: Northwestern University Press.

Weare, K. (2004). *Developing the emotionally literate school*. Los Angeles: Sage.

Chapter Six

Narrative Pedagogy as a Mindful Contemplative Practice

Discovering Preservice Teachers' Mindful Presence

Elsie L. Olan, University of Central Florida, Orlando, Florida, and
Roshmi Mishra, State University of New York at Oswego

Research demonstrates that the current K–12 school system in the United States is one that fosters more "mindlessness" than deep learning, more competitiveness than compassion, and one that favors the head over the heart (Beddoe, 2004; Kyle, 2010; Langer, 1993). In addition, K–12 students are experiencing increasing amounts of stress that impedes their ability to learn, while teachers are being burdened with increasing expectations and decreasing support (Miller & Nozawa, 2005; Napoli, 2004; Gunnlaugson et al., 2014). Kyle claims that "in light of these growing challenges, public educators are seeking alternatives to the traditional ways of approaching education" (2010, p. 1).

How can the implementation of narrative pedagogy as a mindful contemplative practice in a methods course inform preservice teachers' mindful presence?

Goodson and Gill (2011) define narrative pedagogy as the facilitation of an educative journey through which learning takes place in profound encounters, and by engaging in meaning-making and deep dialogue and exchange (p. 123). As Diekelmann and Diekelmann (2009) suggest,

> Narrative pedagogy obtains the on-coming of on-going converging conversations. It calls into question the seemingly self-evident assumptions or pre-

sumptions of all pedagogies. While narrative pedagogy always includes self-mindfulness, it seeks richer understandings of schooling, learning and teaching. Narrative pedagogy is a recovery of the embodied and dialogical experiences of schooling, learning, and teaching as an intra-related phenomenon rather than a series of unrelated neutral activities. (p. xx)

In this quote, Diekelmann and Diekelmann (2009) capture how narrative pedagogy examines the elements in the learning and teaching experience and how it uses awareness and lived experiences as a way to inform teaching practices. Narrative pedagogy as a mindful contemplative practice offers a new and emerging approach for preservice teachers to discover their mindful presence and decision making.

Narrative pedagogy is employed as a conceptual framework where preservice teachers are encouraged to construct knowledge as they revisit their written narratives, experiences, introspective reflections, and dialogic interactions while developing a mindful presence. This chapter draws on research conducted during a longitudinal, yearlong narrative study of 172 preservice teachers' practicum and methods course experiences. It examines narratives preservice teachers wrote about embodying and enacting Rockwell's (2002) "five wisdoms" and displaying "mindful presence" (Miller, 2013).

Throughout this chapter, researchers will demonstrate how the use of narrative pedagogy as a mindful contemplative practice encourages preservice teachers to discover their mindful presence by experiencing introspective reflection, awareness, and Karelaia's (2014) four stages of mindful decision making.

NARRATIVE PEDAGOGY AS A CONTEMPLATIVE PRACTICE

As Thomas Falkenberg (2012) states, contemplative practice is a practice in "which the practitioner is in the state of nonjudgmental, preconceptual conscious awareness of the inner-life experiences in the moment while being engaged in teaching" (p. 31). Narrative pedagogy asserts that knowledge is constructed through awareness, reflection, and dialogical conversations (Goodson & Gill, 2011). Narrative understandings are founded on the observed and recorded actions of everyday lived experiences (Barton, Hamilton, & Ivanic, 2000). Learning is an active and alive engagement that is defined by more than learning a set of skills. Instead, knowledge is negotiated, contested, and enjoined (Gee, 2008) so as to incorporate and define our understanding of the world.

Narratives are examined in order to learn how to appreciate the wider context of preservice teachers' lives, and how these personal stories can illustrate their teacher development and teacher identity formation. Telling a story "makes the moment live beyond the moment" (Riessman, 2008, p. 63).

The telling and revisiting of stories or narrative pedagogy informs preservice teachers' experiences. Olan (2015) states that the use of "descriptive narratives of school experiences can initiate the kinds of conversations and research that is imperative for teacher development and implicit in the everyday trials and tribulations present in educational institutions" (p. 1957).

Preservice teachers' reflections of their school experiences include a sense of awareness and mindful presence. These introspective reflections include an awareness that informs classroom decisions and actions. The awareness and the action is situated in the preservice teachers' past and present lived experiences and their field experiences, which are revealed in their engagement with mindful breathing and contemplative narrative pedagogy. Narrative pedagogy as a contemplative practice contributes to preservice teachers' wisdoms and mindful presence. Goodson and Gill (2011) explain,

> Narrative pedagogy is an invitation to enter another individual's mind, emotions and spirit as well as values, worldviews, traditions, and moral and personal dilemmas. Narrative pedagogy is about showing respect and appreciation for an individual's nature, disposition, talents and aspiration. It also depends on the teacher's ability to identify with the learners as persons and fellow human beings, and to be open to the learners' self-knowledge, current needs, narrative capacities and characters, lived experiences of the past and present, and their capacities for consolidating, modifying and transforming their narratives towards their wellbeing and flourishing. (p. 125)

When preservice teachers experience challenging events and/or situations they cannot immediately resolve, they step back to question and analyze their experiences.

When preservice teachers used narrative pedagogy as a contemplative practice and were afforded time to share their narratives with their classmates, they revisited their assumptions and made decisions regarding their mindful presence and pedagogical practices and beliefs. Many teacher educators use narratives to better understand how personal experiences impact what they believe about teaching and how they engage in practice (Miller, 2005). In this study, the researchers revisited data and identified the crucial role stories occupied in regard to preservice teachers' responses while elucidating introspective reflection, mindful presence, and decision making.

MINDFUL PRESENCE: INTROSPECTIVE REFLECTION, AWARENESS, AND DECISION MAKING

Rockwell's five wisdoms illustrate the qualities of mindfulness. The five wisdoms are awareness, fulfillment, compassion, beneficial activity, and spaciousness (Rockwell, 2002). Kabat-Zinn (2009) describes the essence of mindfulness which is inclusive of Rockwell's five wisdoms as "paying attention in a particular way, on purpose, in the present moment nonjudgmentally" (p. 4). Kabat-Zinn (2009) and Miller (2013) emphasize that self-reflection and acceptance are hallmarks for educators.

The five wisdoms and self-reflection are forms of introspective reflection that help develop a mindful presence. The practice of mindfulness as well as narrative pedagogy as a mindful contemplative practice encourages preservice teachers to engage in introspective reflection. The act of contemplative practices such as mindfulness and narrative pedagogy informs preservice teachers of their reflective stance and how they think about teaching as a practice. Engaging in contemplative narrative pedagogy through seated mindfulness breathing practices, revisiting their stories, and reflective writing allows preservice teachers to experience what Miller identifies as "mindful presence"—to bring about attention and awareness (2013, p. 4).

Karelaia's four stages of mindful decision making also foster the reflective stance of a mindful presence. The four stages help to determine how mindful educators make decisions. The four stages are a) framing the decision, b) gathering ideas and information, c) coming to a conclusion, and d) learning from experience (Karelaia, 2014). Beyond fostering a reflective stance, preservice teachers work toward cultivating mindfulness in order to enhance their mindful presence. As Griggs and Tidwell (2015) note,

> The value of cultivating mindfulness is that it can help one to be more conscious and aware of oneself and one's surroundings on a more continuous basis, partly in the service of being the person one aspires to be, and partly to operate with compassion and empathy more profoundly and more consistently. (p. 90)

It is during this process of cultivating mindfulness that preservice teachers make a conscious effort to practice their breathing, reflect on their decision making, and revisit their stories while displaying a sense of awareness, compassion, and empathy.

METHODOLOGY

Context of Study

Becker and Geer (1957) claim that long-term participant observation provides more complete data about specific situations and events than any other method. A longitudinal study is an observational research method in which data is gathered for the same subjects repeatedly over a period of time. In this longitudinal study, participants were in a university-level preservice teacher education internship experience where they observed and taught lessons for grades six through twelve. Participation was voluntary and the same individuals were observed over a one-year period.

During this study, all preservice teachers engaged in seated mindful breathing techniques. The breathing was sustained for a few minutes at the beginning of the class. The preservice teachers were asked to either close their eyes, gaze downward, or to look at the projection of geometric figures in the form of animated Graphic Interchange Formats (GIFs). The GIFs were used to cue the inhale and the exhale when engaging in mindful breathing.

The GIFs demonstrated a long and slow breath by showing a circle or a hexagon getting larger with the word "inhale" in the center and the circle or hexagon getting smaller with the word "exhale" in it. This was repeated for a few minutes. If the practice involved gazing downward or keeping eyes closed, sometimes a chime was struck by the professor to allow the preservice teacher to mimic the length of their inhale and exhale with the sound.

The professor demonstrated the technique to preservice teachers before the start of the practice and each time the practice occurred. The mindful breathing practice was used to initiate preservice teachers' mindful presence. To follow with the cultivation of preservice teachers' mindful presence, preservice teachers engaged in reflective writing and narrative pedagogy in their education methods course.

A questionnaire was administered to discover how mindfulness can inform preservice teachers' identity and to direct the research. The examination of the 172 preservice teachers' storied responses to the four open-ended questions covered a range of dynamics of learning and embodiment of mindfulness, thereby extending preservice teachers' understanding of their own learning and teaching and the impact this has had on student learning.

Participants

All student names are pseudonyms. The first group of undergraduate preservice teacher candidates were English Language Arts (ELA) majors in secondary education enrolled in a methods course in an urban setting at an American public research university. This university is situated in a diverse setting in the United States.

The second group were undergraduate preservice teachers from a secondary Social Studies Methods class and a secondary Interdisciplinary Methods class. The third group were graduate students in an Elementary Methods class. These participants all attended a public state university situated in a rural setting in the United States.

Data Collection Instruments and Analysis

For this study, a questionnaire of four open-ended questions was created utilizing Karelaia's (2014) four stages of mindful decision making. Preservice teachers answered the following four open-ended questions using Karelia's decision-making framework:

- What is your definition of mindfulness?
- How, if at all, does mindfulness inform your practice as a preservice teacher?
- How, if at all, will mindfulness affect your potential students?
- Please share your stories about mindful teachers. What, if at all, was the impact of the experiences in your learning and teaching?

Preservice teachers engaged in conversations where they reflected on their schooling experiences, learning and teaching, and their professional identity.

The undergraduate ELA preservice teachers worked on crafting narratives where they shared their experiences about their learning, teaching, writing, and the development of a classroom climate. Preservice teachers in the Interdisciplinary Methods course, who did recall having a teacher that they identified as being mindful, expressed that these teachers had more positive feelings associated with them, such as being more caring.

THEMATIC FINDINGS

The examination of the 172 preservice teachers' storied responses to the four open-ended questions demonstrates preservice teachers' understanding of their own learning and teaching, the impact this has on student learning, and their mindful presence. The following themes emerged in highest frequencies in the findings:

a) Eighty-seven percent (151/172) of preservice teachers' storied responses stated that mindful teachers are those who create a positive, beneficial atmosphere for learning and engaging students in class. In his narrative, Brandon remarked that the mindful teachers he has had cultivated a mindful environment and "created a relaxed and open area for students to learn in." He explains that this teacher "seemed to care about all of us, no matter what. I never felt any anxiety coming to school because of the type of class she [the mindful teacher] fostered for us." Brandon's teacher created a class environment of fun where the feeling of safety and inclusiveness prevails.

Another preservice teacher, Rachel, reflects that the best teacher she had was her middle school ELA teacher whom she described as mindful. She described her teacher as one who knew herself very well, and got to know her students just as well. This created a buy-in from the class that had almost every student surpassing previous scores/grades and looking forward to the class. Rachel ends her reflection by stating that she hopes "to be mindful" like her ELA teacher.

This awareness cultivates the use of Karelaia's mindful decision making, and the preservice teacher's mindful presence. By being aware of the mindful qualities of their teachers from their written narratives, the preservice teachers recognized their own mindful presence. Griggs and Tidwell (2015) recognize that mindful teachers incorporate mindful decision making when their teaching is "integrative, reflective and deep" (p. 90).

b) Eighty-six percent (149/172) of preservice teachers' storied responses characterized mindful teachers as understanding and being aware of others' needs. The participants' responses identified how mindful teachers display their mindful presence when they can reflect on how their pedagogical practices inform or impact student learning.

For example, Molly's storied response states that being mindful and having a mindful presence can allow her to do a "better job of reaching my students." Molly discovered her mindful presence by experiencing introspective reflection. This reflection enabled her to recognize that increased awareness can help teachers make more mindful decisions that benefit students. Likewise, Kim discovers that mindfulness would help her better "understand how kids' minds work" while recognizing that her students have concerns and "problems" outside of school that influence their learning.

Kim concluded that "mindful teachers make the classroom environment and students more relaxed." She further comments that this allowed for an "increase in learning, with less of a focus on homework and tests. You could focus on relaxing, that way you could complete the things with less stress." She concludes that this mindful classroom environment allowed her "to feel better and more comfortable."

Nani agreed that "mindfulness has been everything in my practice." She emphasized how learning about the needs of students, and being in touch with how they learn, is everything. She states, "It helps me with my teaching as well as to become a resource for them as they are learning new content."

Nani states that "without mindfulness my students become simple bodies in a chair." She says that during her internship, she observed students that were disengaged and wondered if all of this is due to lack of mindfulness or if this is what classrooms look like and if so then what is my purpose in the classroom? And she reiterates that she "never ever wants to become a teacher that does not care or works without a purpose." Nani's reflective response demonstrated how she unpacked her mindful stance. She alluded to her professional identity as a mindful teacher and in doing so she revisited her internship experiences.

c) Eighty-four percent (146/172) of preservice teachers' storied responses indicated that mindful teachers help to support and care for students. This acknowledges awareness that a mindful presence and mindful decision making can support students' needs. For instance, Scott, a preservice teacher, recognized that thinking about and sharing his understanding of mindfulness informed him to be "more knowledgeable about [his] students' lives and any problems they may have." Scott continues by stating that if he takes into consideration his students' needs, the students "will see me as a mindful teacher and follow my example." His introspective reflection about pedagogical practices and beliefs allows him to use mindfulness to influence his students in a positive manner.

Likewise, Chelsea shared her thoughts about mindful teachers and teaching. She reminisced about Ms. S, a mindful teacher, who was very aware and connected to her students, their lives, and their needs. Chelsea identified that Ms. S created a comfortable and engaging classroom environment for each student. Chelsea states that her experience with Ms. S has "informed her practice as a preservice teacher."

In Chelsea's reflective writings she hopes "to facilitate a more open, comfortable, safe, understanding, accepting and trusting learning environment." She recognizes that her memories of a mindful teacher depict "a teacher that was very aware and connected to her students, their lives, and their needs." Finally, Chelsea remarks that sometimes during the internship experience, "preservice teachers do not see enough mindfulness."

DISCUSSION OF THEMATIC FINDINGS

Examining the thematic findings of the sampled preservice teachers' storied responses, it becomes apparent that mindful teachers are more reflective in both their understanding of their students and their teaching. As Schoeberlein and Sheth (2009) recognize, "a master teacher is a mindful teacher" (p. 1). This is echoed in the way that preservice teachers' narratives reported that mindful teachers consider many aspects of a situation when instituting management strategies with their students and their classroom. It is also clear that a mindful teacher is more reflective and employs better decision-making skills.

Mindful teachers' thoughts and actions are rooted in an awareness of students' best interests as well as supportive learning environments. In a reflective narrative, preservice teacher Brandon recalled how his teacher used mindfulness as a way to create a relaxed classroom environment, one in which students "never felt anxiety coming to school." Brandon's narrative characterizes a teacher whose mindful presence fostered a positive classroom where rapport amongst students and the teacher reigned.

Preservice teachers who had no previous experience with mindfulness recognized that it is a quality that demonstrates a sense of awareness. Mindful teachers can benefit students in the classroom by using their sense of awareness to foster a positive learning environment. Participants' storied responses focused on their experiences with prior teachers, the discovery of their mindful presence, and development of mindful practices.

Overwhelmingly, the sampled groups of preservice teachers reported that mindful teachers strive to create an inclusive, positive, and engaging class environment. In this environment students realize that the teacher is aware of their needs and will seek ways to both model and teach to students' needs in order to foster long-term benefits.

CONCLUSION

The storied responses revealed preservice teachers' perception of mindfulness and their discovery of mindful presence. As preservice teachers shared, revisited, and reflected on their narratives, they began using narrative pedagogy as a mindful contemplative practice. Narrative pedagogy cultivates awareness of self and of the students that preservice teachers will one day teach.

This awareness is what preservice teacher Bethanne explains when she states, "If you are not aware of yourself, you can't expect your students to be aware either." Likewise, Annelise adds that "this awareness allows students to know that their teacher cares about them." Another preservice teacher, Kaisle, suggests that this awareness would "inform the teacher's ability to assist their students."

By utilizing narrative pedagogy as a mindful contemplative practice, teacher educators will begin to answer the questions (a) What is good teaching? (b) How do students learn? and (c) How can teachers motivate students to really think and learn? As Schoeberlein and Sheth (2009) claim, "Mindful teaching nurtures a learning community in which students flourish academically, emotionally, and socially and teachers thrive professionally and personally" (p. 1).

ESSENTIAL IDEAS TO CONSIDER

After analyzing 172 preservice teachers' storied responses and thematically coding the narratives, the following takeaways emerged:

- Narrative pedagogy as a mindful contemplative practice offers a new and emerging approach for preservice teachers to discover their mindful presence and decision making.

- Teachers and preservice teachers should incorporate narrative pedagogy as a contemplative practice in their learning and teaching in order to further discover their mindful presence.
- Teacher educators need to include narrative pedagogy as a contemplative practice in order to help preservice teachers develop a mindful presence, become reflective about their learning and teaching, and make strategic decisions about their classroom instruction.
- Teacher educators can practice mindfulness to help clarify course objectives, generate options, and model mindfulness and a mindful presence.
- The act of contemplative practices such as mindfulness and narrative pedagogy informs preservice teachers of their reflective stance and how they think about teaching as a practice.

REFERENCES

Barton, D., Hamilton, M., & Ivanic, R. (Eds.). (2000). *Situated literacies: Reading and writing in context.* London: Routledge.

Becker, H., & Geer, B. (1957). Participant observation and interviewing: A comparison. *Human Organization, 16*(3), 28–32.

Beddoe, A. E. (2004). Does mindfulness decrease stress and foster empathy among nursing students? *Journal of Nursing Education, 43*(7), 305–312.

Diekelmann, N., & Diekelmann, J. (2009). *Schooling learning teaching: Toward narrative pedagogy.* Bloomington, IN: iUniverse Inc.

Falkenberg, T. (2012). Teaching as contemplative professional practice. *Philosophical Inquiry in Education, 20*(2), 25–35.

Gee, J. P. (2008). *Social linguistics and literacies: Ideology in discourses.* London: Routledge.

Goodson, I., & Gill, S. (2011). *Narrative pedagogy: Life history and learning.* Washington, DC: Peter Lang.

Griggs, T., & Tidwell, D. (2015). Learning to teach mindfully: Examining the self in the context of multicultural education. *Teacher Education Quarterly, 42*(2), 87.

Gunnlaugson, O., Sarath, E. W., Scott, C., & Bai, H. (Eds.). (2014). *Contemplative learning and inquiry across disciplines.* New York: SUNY Press.

Kabat-Zinn, J. (2009). *Wherever you go, there you are: Mindfulness meditation in everyday life.* Boston: Hachette Books.

Karelaia, N. (2014). Why mindful individuals make better decisions. *INSEAD Knowledge.* Retrieved from http://knowledge.insead.edu/leadership-management/why-mindful-individuals-make-better-decisions-3479.

Kyle, E. (2010). Being mindful of mindlessness: An overview of contemplative education programs for secular settings. Proceedings of the Religious Education Association (REA) Annual Meeting, Denver, CO.http://old.religiouseducation.net/proceedings/2010_Proceedings/RIG1.3_Kyle.pdf.

Langer, E. J. (1993). A mindful education. *Educational Psychologist, 28*(1), 43–50.

Miller, J. L. (2005). *Sounds of silence breaking: Women, autobiography, curriculum.* New York: Peter Lang.

Miller, J. P. (2013). *The contemplative practitioner: Meditation in education and the workplace.* Toronto, ON: University of Toronto Press.

Miller, J., & Nozawa, A. (2005). *Contemplative practices in teacher education.* Brandon, VT: Holistic Education Press.

Napoli, M. (2004). Mindfulness training for teachers: A pilot program. *Complementary Health Practice Review, 9*(1), 31–42.

Olan, E. L. (2015). Narratives that inform pre-service secondary English teachers' writing instruction and pedagogy. *Literacy Information and Computer Education Journal, 6*(3), 1956–1963.

Riessman, C. K. (1993). *Narrative analysis.* Newbury Park, CA: Sage.

Riessman, C. K. (2008). *Narrative methods for the human sciences.* Boston: Sage.

Rockwell, I. (2002). *The five wisdoms: A contemplative approach to integrative learning.* New York: Peter Lang Press.

Schoeberlein, D. R., & Sheth, S. (2009). *Mindful teaching and teaching mindfulness: A guide for anyone who teaches anything.* Somerville, MA: Wisdom Publications.

Chapter Seven

Mindfulness, Student Resistance, and the Limits of Fast-Track Teacher Prep

Jennifer Cannon, University of Massachusetts
at Amherst, Amherst, Massachusetts

While mindfulness is rapidly gaining favor in the field of teacher education, in what context(s) and under what circumstances might mindfulness meditation be an unwise pedagogical choice? As mindfulness instructors and contemplative scholars, what can we learn from student resistance? This chapter examines some of the challenges and possibilities of utilizing mindfulness practices in the context of an urban, fast-track teacher preparation program.

The data for this study was gathered in the Fall of 2011 from a required teacher education course, Adolescent Growth and Development. It is significant to note that this course was taught from a social justice framework, which was by instructor choice, not by design of the teacher preparation program. The course was team taught by two white women with extensive social justice training and teaching experience. The author of this chapter was one of the co-instructors for the course and is a UCLA certified mindfulness facilitator.

One of the goals of the course was to foster a broad and culturally nuanced lens for interpreting the topic of adolescent growth and development. The course included a thoughtful exploration of race, class, gender, immigrant status, and the role of the criminal justice system, as these factors profoundly impact the healthy development of children, youth, and families. Utilizing antiracism pedagogy and social justice curricula, the graduate students were provided with a sociopolitical and historical context for understanding systems of oppression.

The decision to teach the course from a social justice framework was informed by the nature of the fast-track teacher preparation program. Like many such programs, the preservice teachers were primarily white and were placed in schools serving majority African American and Latino students. However, the program offered no required course about cultural and racial diversity or multicultural education. As such, the instructors believed it was essential to integrate an analysis of race, class, gender, and structural oppression into the required Adolescent Growth and Development course.

CONTEMPLATIVE FRAMEWORK

The choice to integrate contemplative practices into the course was an attempt to bridge some of the gaps between the intellectual and the emotional, external knowledge and internal knowledge, cognitive thought and embodied awareness. The instructors were interested in how contemplative practices might support or deepen a collective exploration of social justice issues. Knowing the complexity and emotional labor involved with teaching about issues of power, privilege, and oppression, the instructors also wanted to build in reflective and contemplative pauses in the teaching process.

The following contemplative practices were used in the course: mindfulness meditation, loving-kindness meditation, silent journaling, relational mindfulness practices, and contemplative reading exercises. Class began with a five- to ten-minute guided mindfulness meditation, usually beginning and ending with the sound of a bell. Despite initial interest, many of the students came to resist the mindfulness practice. Utilizing student voices, this chapter will begin to make meaning of the resistance, paying careful attention to how structural aspects of the teacher preparation program influenced these outcomes.

CONTEXT AND DATA SOURCES

The context of this study was an intensive two-semester graduate program at a large public university in the Northeast, leading to teacher licensure and a Master's degree in Education. Students in the program were placed in a high-poverty, under-resourced urban public school where they were paired with a mentor teacher. For a good part of the school year, preservice teachers assumed full responsibility for up to three class periods a day while also attending graduate courses in the evening. The course was held once per week for 2.5 hours in a middle school library in the partner school district.

With no summer session attached to the program, all of the required work was completed during the two-semester academic year, placing very high demands on the students' time and emotional energy. Teacher education programs such as this have been referred to as fast-track or boot camp (Friedrich, 2014; Nygreen, Madeloni, & Cannon, 2015) as the programs are a fast-paced, highly demanding, quick route to teacher certification and job placement.

There were twenty-two preservice teachers enrolled in the course who were representative of the teacher population in the United States: predominantly white, middle- to upper-middle class, from suburban backgrounds. Most of the graduate students had little to no experience working with culturally and linguistically diverse youth or communities. Some had no prior experience working with youth at all. Most attended racially homogeneous, majority white, K–12 schools and colleges in New England.

This study can best be understood as a qualitative case study (Bogdan & Biklen, 2003) utilizing ethnographic data collection and practitioner research. As a co-instructor of the course it was nearly impossible to take detailed field notes while simultaneously teaching. As Herr and Anderson (2005) state, "Using the ethnographic approach places practitioners in a logistically untenable position because they can't work and record data at the same time" (p. 34). Therefore, the use of reflective diaries, journals, or practitioner memos becomes essential for practitioner researchers.

The following data sources were collected over a period of four months from September to December 2011: field notes; practitioner memos; audio-recorded debriefing sessions with co-instructor immediately following each class; lesson plans and classroom materials; student papers and online blog posts; emails from students and between instructors; student surveys; extensive participatory midsemester and final course evaluations.

FINDINGS: THEMES OF RESISTANCE

The following sections will focus on the theme of resistance as expressed by the students in five subthemes: discomfort with silence; structural limitations of the teacher prep program; white privilege; applicability or transferability of mindfulness practices to secondary school settings; and the perception of mindfulness as a spiritual practice. The chapter will then briefly explore relational mindfulness practices, which were embraced, in addition to contemplative practices such as silent journaling and contemplative poetry reading.

Discomfort with Silence

Several students expressed discomfort with the silence during the meditations, a reaction that is not uncommon for first-time meditators (see Dorman, 2015; Kabat-Zinn, 2013). The following are excerpts from the instructor's field notes dated September 7, 2011:

> One student shared that she is from a large Italian and Irish Catholic family where there is never any silence or alone-space. She said the meditation made her uncomfortable and she couldn't wait for it to be over. Another student said she felt giddy and wanted to laugh during the meditation—it reminded her of being in church when you are supposed to be quiet.

As the comments above indicate, the discomfort may have to do with cultural or family norms related to silence. Perhaps more apparent, we live in a fast-paced, highly technological culture where little attention is given to the values of silence and introspection. Students are habituated to filling spare moments with cell phones, emails, text messages, tweets and Facebook updates, and are socialized to find relaxation through video games, movies, and TV shows.

Structural Limitations: Fast-track Teacher Prep

Another theme of resistance to the mindfulness practice had to do with the enormous amount of stress preservice teachers were facing in a fast-track program in which participants earned a Master's degree of Education and a license to teach in 180 days. The students were required to co-instruct with a mentor teacher five days a week throughout the school year while staying current with graduate level classes. The feelings of anxiety, exhaustion, and overwhelm were apparent during class. While some students responded with genuine appreciation for the moments of quiet meditation, other students responded with increased anxiety or even anger.

The midterm evaluations revealed that many students did not view the mindfulness practice as an effective use of class time. The comments requested more time to discuss the assigned readings and more time on teaching methods, despite the fact that the class was not a methods course. The following is an excerpt taken from the midterm evaluations:

> I think the instructors could benefit from understanding the position of the cohort. Many members have felt overwhelmed and are desperate for practical resources. Also, many members of the cohort are in "survival mode."

The students talked about their teacher training as if they were going through a military boot camp; they routinely referenced sleep deprivation, being in a constant state of anxiety, and not having enough time for basic self-care. These are some of the consequences of a fast-track teacher prep program. Given these limitations, the instructors began to question if students had the capacity to engage with mindfulness practices when they were in survival mode. The following excerpt is from the student online blog about contemplative practice:

> The entire time I am sitting there, worried over the lesson plans I have to write, the papers that need grading, the other grad homework that needs to get done. It's very frustrating to have to endure my precious time being wasted. At another time, in another setting, when I don't have so many people pulling me in so many different directions, might mindfulness be useful and relevant? Maybe. It's something to consider, and now that I know it exists, I will keep this thought in the back of my head. But I think it's time to move on now.

The preservice teachers shared a common desire to fill the silence with words, and expressed an urgent need to fill every moment of class time with knowledge and content, as seen in this excerpt:

> I find that this mindfulness practice bothers me more than it helps me because time is so precious at this point in my life. I understand the value of slowing down and appreciating things "in the moment," but all that happens in my brain when I sit quietly for 8–10 minutes is chaos. I am constantly thinking of the load of work that I have to do, and it feels as though we could be using that time a bit more valuably.

The implicit assumption is that knowledge is not produced from silence or generated in contemplative states of awareness. Traditional education reinforces a transfer of knowledge from teacher to student, as in a banking model of education (Freire, 1970). In our methods-dominated teacher education programs, the emphasis on how to teach is driven by standardized curriculum and high-stakes testing (Berlak, 2011; Madeloni & Gorlewski, 2013), especially in low-performing schools where teachers are under tremendous pressure to raise test scores (Au, 2009; Hursh, 2009; Taubman, 2009).

Many of the preservice teachers felt a sense of panic, given the overwhelming demands of the fast-track teacher prep program. They did not feel as if there was enough time for mindfulness practices or social justice theoretical content that did not apply *directly* to their daily challenges as secondary teachers. Both were seen as nonessential.

The graduate students routinely asked for teaching methods and disciplinary tools that would help them manage student behavior and reach the expectations of school administration under pressure from the state. For many of them, the mindfulness practices served to highlight the stress, anxiety, and panic they were feeling about completing their workload and becoming effective teachers.

White Privilege

Teacher educator Leigh Patel (in Patel et al., 2013) writes about the successful integration of mindfulness practices in her teacher education course, as a woman of color teaching mostly preservice teachers of color in an urban context. Her intention in utilizing mindfulness practices was to create a humanizing pedagogy (Freire, 1970) in her classroom. Patel's students seemed to share a social justice orientation and were open and receptive to exploring contemplative practices as a liberatory process, in other words, a praxis of liberation as opposed to stress-reduction (see Berila, 2016; Rendón, 2009).

In contrast, the preservice teachers in this study were predominantly white and were encountering antiracist pedagogy and social justice theory for the first time. Many of the students expressed resistance to the course content that included issues of institutional racism, white privilege, classism, colonialism, and English language hegemony. This was not a surprising finding as this phenomenon is well theorized in the literature about antiracist education (DiAngelo, 2012; Garrett & Segall, 2013; Howard, 2006; Picower, 2009; Tatum, 2003).

Drawing from field notes and practitioner memos, the following examples of white privilege help to illustrate the classroom climate. Several of the white graduate students did not feel safe in the communities of color in which they were teaching, creating (unexamined) anxiety and fear.

Many members of the cohort held deficit views (Valencia, 1997) of the parents of their middle and high school students, citing violence, drug addiction, poverty, and crime as examples of their low morality and lack of investment in their children's education. Some members of the cohort described their immersion in the urban school environment as a cross-cultural adventure akin to the Peace Corps, using the analogy of being dropped into a foreign land with accompanying culture shock.

White privilege was also expressed through a discourse of charity and benevolence, a desire to "do good" and make a difference in some of our nation's lowest performing schools, while simultaneously resisting a closer examination of the historical and sociopolitical conditions that created the current public school crisis in many communities of color. This is not to say that every member of the graduate cohort was defensive about institutional racism; however, the overall climate was driven by deficit thinking and variations of the white savior trope (Hughey, 2014).

In this particular context, an invitation to slow down and tune in to one's inner emotional climate, via mindfulness practices, was a recipe to encounter difficult emotions associated with unlearning privilege (Berila, 2016). While this exploration was one of our pedagogical aims, many of the preservice teachers felt this was not a productive use of class time.

Applicability of Mindfulness to Secondary Teaching Context

Another area of resistance emerged in the form of questioning the applicability of mindfulness to their secondary teaching context. The mindfulness practice was not intended for replication in secondary school classrooms without adequate training. Despite this framing, many of the preservice teachers were focused on how mindfulness could be used as a teaching method or disciplinary tool. As a result, the practice was evaluated and judged in terms of its transferability to their classroom teaching as seen in the following excerpts from student writing:

- I do not see the practical application of this practice, despite having viewed all of the YouTube clips and reviewing the material [about mindfulness] that was assigned in class. I recently read the post about treating us as learners in the classroom rather than teachers, and I appreciate this sentiment. However, I feel that I am pressed for time and am in this program to learn how to teach. I understand also that as a teacher, I am a lifelong learner, but I still wish that I could see some direct application to my rowdy 9th grade class.
- I think it [mindfulness] is very valuable but doubt my ability to pull it off in my own classroom.
- If mindfulness will help students with ADHD or anxiety, then I am open to the idea of it. Yet, I do not see myself using it in my classroom.

Critical scholars have recently raised concerns that mindfulness can be used as a technocratic tool in P–12 education, specifically as a means to increase standardized test scores and manage student behavior (Forbes, 2012; Hsu, 2013). Forbes (2015) argues that mindfulness should not be used in the school system to promote acceptance of a market-driven reform agenda that is causing harm to our children and teachers. Given the fraught dynamics of race and racism in our public schools, it would be prudent for teachers to exercise caution in terms of using mindfulness as a behavior management tool, especially white teachers in communities of color (Cannon, 2016). It was for this myriad of complicated reasons that the instructors chose not to teach mindfulness as a technique for the preservice teachers to replicate in their secondary classrooms.

Mindfulness as a Spiritual Practice

Some of the students expressed resistance to the mindfulness practice by claiming it was too religious or spiritual. One class session, in particular, elicited a strong response from several students. The mindfulness practice followed a class discussion about the impending execution of Troy Davis, an African American man on death row. The execution had gained international attention and was scheduled on September 21, 2011, the same evening as class. Despite a full agenda for the day, the instructors felt that it was critical to talk about the case as the cohort was preparing to teach in communities that had been devastated by institutional racism and incarceration (Alexander, 2010).

On this particular day of class, the instructors opened with a dialogue about the case and made connections to the local community. The instructors were stunned by the pushback they received, including one accusation of reverse racism. Without adequate historical context and an anti-racist analysis, the students had been socialized to support the white-dominated criminal justice system, and more importantly, they had been trained not to question the status quo, including the rates of incarceration for African American and Latino men. After the Troy Davis dialogue the class proceeded with the weekly mindfulness meditation.

The next week the instructors opened class by talking about Troy Davis and his execution by the state of Georgia. The following excerpt, taken from the instructor's field notes, captures the reaction of two students:

> Natalie spoke up first and said that several people in the class were uncomfortable with the way I led the mindfulness meditation last week. They felt like I was forcing them to take a moment of silence for Troy Davis. Russell, an Afghanistan war veteran and ex–police officer, expressed that he was uncomfortable with the meditation because it felt too close to prayer. He said we discussed the Troy Davis case and then went right into a meditation that felt leading. (September 29, 2011)

In hindsight, it would have been more effective to begin class with a brief mindfulness meditation and then follow with a dialogue about the Troy Davis case. Because the instructors' personal views about the injustice of the execution were clear, some of the students felt like the meditation was being offered as a moment of silence for Troy Davis, even though that was not the intention. Upon reflection, the instructors wondered if the same kind of resistance would have arisen from students of color who may have welcomed a moment of meditation after talking about Troy Davis.

The dialogue about mindfulness practice continued and another student voiced his opinion. The following excerpt is taken from the instructor's field notes:

> Stephen commented that the meditation walks a fine line with religion and spirituality. He pointed out a Tibetan prayer bell I was using as a chime and my reference to teaching as a "sacred craft." (September 29, 2011)

This comment created a hypervigilance in the teaching team about separating secular mindfulness from anything that could be seen as spiritual. The bell was not a Tibetan prayer bell, but the instructors stopped using it nonetheless. This exchange with the students highlighted how vulnerable it is to take pedagogical risks in the classroom. It was a pedagogical risk to talk about the execution of Troy Davis, and also a risk to lead mindfulness meditation. Doing both on the same day, the meditation following the controversial Troy Davis discussion, was particularly risky.

RELATIONAL CONTEMPLATIVE PRACTICES: CONNECTING FROM THE HEART

While several students looked forward to the silent meditation at the beginning of class, many students expressed their discomfort with the practice as outlined in the sections above. At the midterm, it became clear that the instructors needed to shift the approach, and consequently, the mindfulness meditation practice was stopped. As an alternative, the instructors began to integrate relational contemplative practices, such as mindful listening and speaking in pairs, in addition to other contemplative exercises.

Before viewing a film about colonial education and Native American boarding schools, the instructors informed the students that they would engage with a contemplative writing practice at the conclusion of the film. The instructors asked for everyone's cooperation with maintaining two minutes of silence immediately following the film. After sitting together in silence (no bell or meditation instructions), the students were asked to free write about whatever they were feeling, trying as best as they were able to connect with their emotions. They were not given any restrictions in terms of writing format.

One of the students volunteered to share her writing and cried openly about her grief and anger connected to our nation's legacy of genocide and racism. She also made insightful connections to present day conditions in the Puerto Rican and African American community where she was teaching. The contemplative exercise helped allow space for her tears and created a climate that honored vulnerability and sharing from the heart.

During another class, the students engaged in a contemplative poetry reading practice using Martin Espada's (1990) poem, "Jorge the Church Janitor Finally Quits." After slowly reading the poem aloud three times, each time followed by a contemplative pause, the students were guided in a silent journaling period. The class dialogue that followed was one of the richest and most productive of the semester as the class talked about cultivating an orientation toward seeing the unseen—recognizing the humanity and worth of all workers in the schools where they were teaching, including custodians, cafeteria workers, and other service employees.

The contemplative poetry reading elicited strong emotion as one student shared his shame about walking past the school's service workers without acknowledging them or making any effort to learn their names, as if they didn't exist. It was the combination of Espada's powerful poem, the contemplative exercise, and the collective exploration of racism that created a transformative learning moment for the class.

CONCLUSION

Understanding and analyzing the context and climate of teacher education programs is vital before implementing mindfulness or contemplative practices as pedagogical tools. Due to the structural limitations of fast-track teacher preparation programs, some mindfulness practices may increase anxiety for preservice teachers who are already experiencing extreme stress. Several students in this study expressed agitation and discomfort when sitting in meditation as they became more aware of their intolerable feelings associated with a high-pressure teacher preparation program.

Many of the students expressed discomfort with silence and also articulated a desire to utilize every minute of class time to learn teaching methods that would be *directly* transferable to their secondary classrooms. The climate of resistance was also due, in part, to the challenging course content, especially the social justice curriculum that required students to engage in a process of self-reflection about privilege and oppression.

This study revealed that relational mindfulness practices were more readily welcomed than silent and guided meditation. Contemplative practices, such as contemplative writing and contemplative poetry reading, were also embraced and served to create a classroom climate where head and heart knowledge could be integrated.

These relational practices allowed students to connect with each other and interrupted a sense of isolation. As mindfulness becomes increasingly popular in teacher education programs, let us collectively engage in productive dialogues about the pedagogical purpose of these practices and the sociopolitical context in which they are being offered.

ESSENTIAL IDEAS TO CONSIDER

- Understanding and analyzing the context and climate of teacher education programs is vital before implementing mindfulness or contemplative practices as pedagogical tools.
- Due to the structural limitations of fast-track teacher prep programs, some mindfulness practices may increase anxiety for preservice teachers who are already experiencing extreme stress.
- Relational mindfulness practices may be more effective than silent and/or guided meditation in certain teacher education programs.

REFERENCES

Alexander, M. (2010). *The new Jim Crow: Mass incarceration in the age of colorblindness.* New York: New Press.

Au, W. (2009) *Unequal by design: High-stakes testing and the standardization of inequality.* New York: Routledge.

Berila, B. (2016). *Integrating mindfulness into anti-oppression pedagogy.* New York: Routledge.

Berlak, A. (2011). Standardized teacher performance assessment: Obama/Duncan's quick fix for what they think it is that ails us. In P. Carr and B. Porfilio (Eds.), *The phenomenon of Obama and the agenda for education* (pp. 187–209). Charlotte, NC: Information Age Publishing.

Bogdan, R., & Biklen, S. (2003). *Qualitative research for education: An introduction to theories and methods.* (4th ed.). New York: Pearson Education Group.

Cannon, J. (2016). Education as the practice of freedom: A social justice proposal for mindfulness educators. In R. E. Purser, D. Forbes, & A. Burke (Eds.), *Handbook of mindfulness: Culture, context, and social engagement* (pp. 397–409). Switzerland: Springer International Publishing.

DiAngelo, R. (2012, February). Nothing to add: The role of white silence in racial discussions. *Understanding and Dismantling Privilege, 2*(2), 1–17.

Dorman, E. H. (2015). Building teachers' social-emotional competence through mindfulness practices. *Curriculum and Teaching Dialogue, 17*(1–2), 103–119.

Espada, M. (1990). *Rebellion is the circle of a lover's hands.* Willimantic, CT: Curbstone Press.

Forbes, D. (2012, June 30). Occupy mindfulness. *Beams & Struts.* Retrieved from http://beamsandstruts.com/articles/item/982-occupy-mindfulness.

Forbes, D. (2015, November 8). They want kids to be robots: Meet the new education craze designed to distract you from overtesting. *Salon.* Retrieved from http://www.salon.com/2015/11/08/they_want_kids_to_be_robots_meet_the_new_education_craze_designed_to_distract_you_from_overtesting/.

Freire, P. (1970). *Pedagogy of the oppressed.* New York: Continuum International Publishing Group.

Friedrich, D. (2014). We brought it upon ourselves: University-based teacher education and the emergence of boot-camp-style routes to teacher certification. *Education Policy Analysis Archives, 22*(2).

Garrett, H. J., & Segall, A. (2013). (Re)considerations of ignorance and resistance in teacher education. *Journal of Teacher Education, 64*(4), 294–304.

Herr, K., & Anderson, G. (2005). *The action research dissertation: A guide for students and faculty.* Thousand Oaks, CA: Sage.

Howard, G. (2006). *We can't teach what we don't know: White teachers, multiracial classrooms.* New York: Teachers College Press.

Hsu, F. (2013, November 4). *The heart of mindfulness: A response to the* New York Times. Retrieved from http://www.buddhistpeacefellowship.org/the-heart-of-mindfulness-a-response-to-the-new-york-times/.

Hughey, M. (2014). *The white savior film: Content, critics and consumption.* Philadelphia: Temple University Press.

Hursh, D. (2009). Assessing "No Child Left Behind" and the rise of neoliberal education policies. *American Educational Research Journal, 44*(3), 493–518.

Kabat-Zinn, J. (2013). *Full catastrophe living: Using the wisdom of your body and mind to face stress, pain, and illness* (2nd ed.). New York: Bantam.

Madeloni, B., & Gorlewski, J. (2013). Wrong answer to the wrong question: Why we need critical teacher education, not standardization. *Rethinking Schools, 27*(4).

Nygreen, K., Madeloni, B., & Cannon, J. (2015). "Boot camp" teacher certification and neoliberal education reform. In K. Sturges (Ed.), *Neoliberalizing educational reform: America's quest for profitable market-colonies and the undoing of public good* (pp. 101–121). Rotterdam, The Netherlands: SensePublishers.

Patel, L., Atkins-Patterson, K., Healy, D., Haralson, J. G., Rosario, L., & Shi, J. (2013). Mindfulness as method: Teaching for connection in a dehumanizing context. *Poverty & Race, 22*(3), 5–13.

Picower, B. (2009). The unexamined whiteness of teaching: How white teachers maintain and enact dominant racial ideologies. *Race, Ethnicity, and Education, 12*(2), 197–215.

Rendón, L. (2009). *Sentipensante (sensing/thinking) pedagogy: Educating for wholeness, social justice and liberation.* Sterling, VA: Stylus Publishing.

Tatum, B. (2003). *Why are all the black kids sitting together in the cafeteria: And other conversations about race.* New York: Basic Books.

Taubman, P. (2009). *Teaching by numbers: Deconstructing the discourse of standards and accountability in education.* New York: Routledge.

Valencia, R. (1997). Conceptualizing the notion of deficit thinking. In R. Valencia (Ed.), *The evolution of deficit thinking* (pp. 1–12). London: Falmer Press.

Chapter Eight

Nurturing the Inner Core through the Five Dimensions of Engaged Teaching

Elizabeth Hope Dorman, Fort Lewis College, Durango, Colorado

Throughout my eighteen years as a teacher educator, I have noticed that preservice teachers are becoming increasingly concerned about entering a profession in which the often high-pressure environments of schools and teacher evaluation systems linked to student academic performance are the norm. These prospective teachers often are stressed and wondering how they will be able to stay centered, grounded, and steeped in well-being once they become teachers of record and have their own classrooms.

Preservice teachers need to develop adequate skills and dispositions to live balanced, satisfying lives as educators, while facing these tensions. Their discernment about what is most deeply meaningful to them, even within the context of busy, pressured lives as college students preparing to be educators, becomes essential to their preparation. As prospective teachers learn to be aware of and pay attention to the inner dimensions of their lives—the *inner core* (Michalec, 2013)—and to apply that self-wisdom in their careers with their own P–12 students, they support their own sustainability and longevity as educators.

Contemplative practices and pedagogy have become integrated into both instruction and curriculum design as a way to work toward these intentions, framed by the question, "What might it look like to help preservice teachers learn how to negotiate the tensions of uncovering and staying true to their inner selves while the outer demands of the teaching profession tug at them vigorously?"

One of the central tools I employ with students to curate attention to their inner lives is a framework called the Five Dimensions of Engaged Teaching

(Weaver & Wilding, 2013). This chapter provides an overview of this frame-work, how and why it is integrated into preservice teacher education, and synthesizes three years of data from interviews and written work to assess the reported impacts of this approach.

INNER CORE IDENTITY WORK

As Paul Michalec conceptualized in 2013, preservice teachers are wrestling with how to maintain their *inner core* while working in the context of the *common core*. Michalec's term "inner core" refers to the inner dimensions of teaching and learning to teach, including but not limited to qualities such as emotion, affect, dispositions, heart, and self-knowing. On the other hand, the "common core" is "shorthand for standards-based reform and teacher ac-countability," including the Common Core State Standards (Michalec, 2013, p. 29).

Fostering contemplative reflection on these elements of identity facilitates teacher candidates' cultivation of their *inner core*. As Greene and Kim (2014) state, an important "purpose of our work with new teachers is to remind them who they are, to empower them with a realization of their core strengths, and to give them the experience of connecting with their strengths" (p. 103).

Michalec argues that the qualities and awareness comprising the inner core are just as valuable as more technical and content-based forms of knowledge that preservice teachers need to develop in order to be effective and satisfied as teaching professionals. The inner core "is noticeable in the authenticity and instructional presence that teacher candidates embody as effective and caring teachers" (Michalec, 2013, p. 31). Contemplation on the inner dimensions of one's life has the potential to lead to teacher authenticity and presence, as one's inner and outer worlds become aligned, undivided, and coherent.

Preservice teachers need opportunities to cultivate their inner core and to learn that good teaching goes *beyond* the "what" and "how" of content and method to the "why" and "who" of purposes of schooling and the question of "who is the self who teaches?" (Palmer, 2007). As Palmer reminds us,

> As important as methods may be, the most practical thing we can achieve in any kind of work is insight into what is happening inside us as we do it. The more familiar we are with our inner terrain, the more surefooted our teach-ing—and living—becomes. (p. 5)

As educators pay attention to the inner dimensions of teaching and of themselves as teachers—what Palmer (1997) calls *the teacher within*—they are indeed engaging in the deep contemplative work of identity construction, of uncovering "who is the self who teaches?"

One central element of self is *authenticity*. Scholars in the field of adult education helped to construct a common understanding of the meanings of authenticity in teaching. As Kreber and her colleagues (Kreber et al., 2007) write in a comprehensive literature review,

> Authenticity in teaching involves features such as being genuine; becoming more self-aware; being defined by one's self rather than by other's expectations; bringing parts of oneself into interactions with students; and critically reflecting on self, others, relationships and context, and so forth. . . . Authenticity is not just something that exclusively rests within myself . . . for authenticity to be meaningful, it needs to be sought in relation to issues that *matter crucially*. (pp. 40–41)

The important work of uncovering one's authentic self and acting in ways consistent with that self-knowledge takes diligent, sustained effort (Weimer, 2011). This inner work is particularly relevant when preparing educators to teach effectively in the highly diverse contexts of twenty-first-century schooling, where they need to be aware of the multiple dimensions of their own social identities (e.g., race, ethnicity, socioeconomic class, gender and sexual orientation, religious beliefs) and those of their P–12 students as well as the various implications of these identities.

THE FIVE DIMENSIONS OF ENGAGED TEACHING: A CONTEMPLATIVE FRAMEWORK

In an effort to cultivate a contemplative and meaningful approach to teacher development that promotes educators' engagement in the identity work of exploring and developing their *inner core*, and aligning their actions to their authentic selves, I integrate the framework of *The Five Dimensions of Engaged Teaching: A Practical Guide for Educators* (2013), by Laura Weaver and Mark Wilding, into all of my courses. The five dimensions can be summarized as follows (Weaver & Wilding, p. 13) and apply to teachers as well as their own students:

- *Cultivating an open heart*: "Expressing warmth, kindness, care, compassion"; cultivating relationships (teacher-student and student-student) and trust in the classroom;
- *Engaging the self-observer*: "Noticing, observing, and reflecting on our thoughts, beliefs, biases, emotions, and behaviors to lead to more conscious actions";

- *Being present*: "Bringing attention to the present moment and learning to manage distractions so we can be responsive, aware, focused, and creative in the classroom";
- *Establishing respectful boundaries*: "Respectfully establishing clear and compassionate boundaries for ourselves and with others";
- *Developing emotional capacity*: "Developing emotional intelligence, expanding our emotional range, and cultivating emotional boundaries so we can effectively address a range of feelings in ourselves and others."

These dimensions represent a fundamental way that a contemplative approach is built into my pedagogy. A common feature of contemplative pedagogy is that learners have opportunities to bridge their inner and outer worlds through inquiry and introspection of various forms, thereby creating "opportunities for greater connection and insight" (e.g., Barbezat & Bush, 2014, p. 5; Palmer, 1997).

Students explore each dimension and investigate their meaning in the fabric of their inner lives through a range of experiential, contemplative practices: mindfulness meditation focused on breathing, sensory awareness, body sensations, thoughts, emotions; centering exercises; relational practices such as mindful listening and dialogue; compassion exercises; journaling; beholding.

The five dimensions are taught explicitly as content and are also frequently used as an anchor to facilitate teacher candidates' reflection on other core concepts of the course or its experiential field study component in classrooms. These sample prompts are designed to foster introspection on the five dimensions and their potential usefulness:

- In what ways are these dimensions meaningful to you in your personal and professional lives at this point in time?
- How would you "rate" yourself on each dimension at this moment in your development? Which come most naturally to you, and which are more challenging for you?
- How can we deliberately cultivate and develop these dimensions in ourselves? In our students?
- In what situations and contexts have you noticed yourself (or others) demonstrating these dimensions (in class, field studies, conversations)?
- How can these dimensions help us deepen our understanding and implementation of culturally responsive pedagogy and multicultural education?
- How do these dimensions explicitly connect to our prior reading, conversations, and other course activities?
- In what ways do we engage these dimensions as a community of learners in this course?

Teacher candidates also consider the five dimensions during their field study interactions and subsequent written reflections, thus joining their inner and outer worlds. For example, they consider what embodied reactions and responses they noticed that day in their interactions with P–12 students, classmates, or mentor teachers.

What physical sensations did they notice in their bodies when a student would not stop having a side conversation during whole-class instructional time? What thoughts, emotions, and associated bodily feelings arose when a student responded with genuine gratitude when offered individual help? This kind of embodied knowing through awareness and reflection is an essential type of self-knowledge for prospective teachers to develop.

METHODOLOGY

To understand preservice teachers' attitudes and perceptions of the Five Dimensions of Engaged Teaching and their views of the impacts of the integration of this framework, self-report data has been collected over three years from ten courses (five iterations of a teaching methods course and five iterations of an equity and diversity course, for a total of 120 students). The preservice teachers who produced the written work excerpted below come from a variety of racial and ethnic groups, with slightly more females than males represented overall.

The students' written work covered a broad range of topics related to the Five Dimensions of Engaged Teaching, including but not limited to responses to the bulleted prompts listed above; reflections on what aspects of the framework they felt most drawn to and how they might apply the concepts in their own future classrooms; how, specifically, the framework helped them pay attention to and process certain strong emotional and physical reactions to P–12 students, classmates, and others in their coursework and field placements; and how, if at all, they were using the five dimensions in their life outside the classroom.

The other major data source informing this ongoing study is a set of semi-structured interviews with seventeen former students who volunteered to talk with me after completing the equity and diversity course. Individual interviews lasted about an hour and focused on preservice teachers' attitudes and perceptions of the five dimensions and their perceived impact on the teacher candidates. The interviews probed deeply into how the five dimensions framework allowed them to access and process the content of the equity and diversity course, specifically the highly-charged emotions that inevitably arise when engaging with that potentially sensitive content. All seventeen interviews were digitally recorded and transcribed verbatim.

Data analysis has been iterative and ongoing in this qualitative, longitudinal study. Early analysis included coding of passages and writing reflective memos to identify emerging themes and patterns (Creswell, 2013; Newby, 2014; Saldaña, 2012). Much of the descriptive coding was guided directly by the interview questions and reflective prompts (for example, "Which of the five dimensions feel most relevant and meaningful to you as a prospective teacher, and why?"). Coded items were then categorized according to themes. Interpretative assertions were written using Erickson's (1986) methods.

Over the three years this study has been in process, adjustments have been made to how the five dimensions have been integrated and explored in courses, guided by ongoing results in an action research framework. The results reported in this chapter represent a current understanding of the findings.

COMMON THEMES FROM DATA ANALYSIS

Theme One: Helpful Framework and Language

Overall, preservice teachers have responded very positively to the infusion of the Five Dimensions of Engaged Teaching into the curriculum. Although the ideas were not always necessarily new to study participants, analysis suggests that the framework and language were particularly useful for them in developing their inner core. For example, a former student who was interviewed months after she had completed my courses said, "The *concepts* have really stuck with me, but the *labels* have fallen aside."

Another participant expressed,

> I really value [the five dimensions], but I think I value them because I already am familiar with them and appreciate them. If I didn't know what they were and I just read "engage the self-observer, be present," I wouldn't really get it . . . it's not something you can read about in a textbook and think that you get it; it's something that you have to *experience* for every single one of these, repeatedly.

This same teacher candidate noted that encountering the five dimensions in the equity course "was really helpful" and "in my opinion, the foundation of teaching, because the content and curriculum doesn't happen well without the emotional relationship. It was reassuring to learn that in multicultural education, these things are valued."

These examples are representative of what the majority of participants shared in writing and in interviews. Essentially, many of them expressed that to some extent they were aware of the importance of the inner dimensions of self, such as emotions, self-awareness, heart, and affect, cultivated by the five dimensions framework.

However, the text itself as well as the related experiential exercises, discussions, and contemplative reflections appear to have equipped them with the language and experiential understanding to communicate about their inner core, and the connections between their inner and outer worlds, in a deeper way.

Theme Two: Authenticity

The engaged teaching framework appears to have allowed preservice teachers to develop their authenticity by facilitating self-awareness; creating confidence in aligning their actions with their values; bringing their full expressions of being into their interactions with peers and students; forging meaningful connections between the subject matter and their own interests; and engaging in critical reflection.

Authenticity is a central aspect of the inner core. As they blend their inner and outer worlds and negotiate their identities in alignment with their true selves, educators are more likely to feel a sense of balance and well-being. As one teacher candidate wrote,

> One thing I found both interesting and helpful was the idea that I am allowed to be imperfect. It's hugely inspiring to me to know that I'm allowed to be human; to have flaws, and idiosyncrasies, and be better at some things than others.

Many participants noted that the specific dimensions of being present and engaging the self-observer in particular fostered their authentic identity development. This idea is expressed in the following passage from an interview:

> Engaging the self-observer and being present are skills for the whole world, and I think that's what leads us to some sort of satisfaction as humans, much beyond teaching. I mean, I don't think engaging the self-observer or being present is something that you can just like do as a *teacher*; it's something that changes the way that you interact with yourself and with the world.

Over and over, preservice teachers talked about being present and engaging the self-observer as core touchstones in their emerging identity development not only as educators but as human beings.

Another teacher candidate spoke specifically about how being present and engaging the self-observer helped her identify ways in which she was not honoring her authentic path by keeping a particular job that kept her up until the middle of the night. The job was making it extremely difficult to be present and engaged for her teacher education courses and field experiences in classrooms, "interfering with my mental state and health," as she put it. Being present and engaging the self-observer, she noted, were new tools that encouraged her to quit that job and define her life on her own terms in a more sustainable approach. As she described,

> Being present helped me also stay focused on things because I'm the type of person that has multiple things going on in their mind. Sometimes I just stop, take a deep breath, and then say, "Okay, this is what I need to be doing right now. . . . Other stuff, I can worry about that later. I don't have to worry about it right now." That helped me in the classroom, that helped me with home-work. . . . It helps me with a lot of things because I get distracted very easily, but now I can just take a deep breath and just keep going.

Participants reported that the engaged teaching framework has allowed them to relax into being human, into truly being who they are, as they test out their authentic identity both in classrooms and in their personal lives. Developing the skills of "using self-knowledge to establish one's own identity" (Kreber et al., 2007; Weimer, 2011, p. 1) is a vital facet of authenticity. These qualities are especially relevant in the current high-stakes accountability context of schooling with such a strong focus on standardization.

It is perhaps not surprising that so many study participants reported connecting in such a meaningful way with the dimensions of being present and engaging the self-observer. Some element of silence and inner listening is needed in order to nurture one's inner core and allow authenticity to emerge. Most of the preservice teachers are twentysomethings who have grown up as digital natives. For them and many of us in this twenty-first-century world of technological distraction and 24/7 connectivity, staying focused on the present moment is a challenge, but something they know is valuable for cultivating their inner core, once they get used to it. As another student wrote,

> I realized how bad I am at staying in the present. I am absolutely horrible at it; I always have so many things running through my mind and find myself rather distracted throughout the day. I am always thinking about what needs to be done and how I am going to do it.
>
> If I am too busy worrying about my day and not being in the present, then how am I supposed to expect my students to do the same? If I am not in the present I am going to miss out on experiences, connecting with my students, and teachable moments that could define what I am teaching in my classroom. By taking advantage of the activities for mindfulness [that we learned], I should be able to build my mental ability to stay in the present.

Developing the ability to notice the tendency of one's mind to wander is a precious gift and can connect us with our authentic selves in the present moment, keeping us from getting caught up in various kinds of worry and anxiety. As described in Killingsworth and Gilbert (2010), we feel more of a sense of well-being when our minds and bodies are in the same place at the same time. The particular dimensions of being present and engaging the self-observer help preservice teachers develop that skill, and in doing so, foster their authenticity as a key aspect of the inner core.

The five dimensions provide preservice teachers with specific tools for allowing themselves to express vulnerability and expand emotional range, important facets of one's inner life. These skills are especially valuable when discussing heated or sensitive topics, as is often the case in the equity course. Preservice teachers cited the dimensions of cultivating an open heart and developing emotional capacity as particularly useful in helping them to become more aware of and comfortable with a broader spectrum of feelings, and ultimately, to develop a deeper sense of themselves as human beings.

One teacher candidate's frank reflections on his awareness of his comfort level with various feelings are expressed through this passage:

> I found that the emotions I tend to feel comfortable with are happiness, excitement, frustration, and conflict; however, I tend to reject sadness and anger because I feel that they make me too vulnerable. Although I know vulnerability is a key aspect to connecting with your students, this feels very risky to me and I must learn to let my guard down and find the right balance of emotions.

In a similar vein, another teacher candidate commented honestly on his lack of ease and skill in working with a particular emotion when he wrote the following:

> I am comfortable dealing with most emotions except sadness. I do not know how to deal with people when they are extremely sad or crying. I need to work on this because I do not want my students feeling like I do not care about them and their problems. I have to look at myself and ask why this emotion makes me uncomfortable so I can work with others and their emotions.

As illustrated in these two passages, the engaged teaching framework appears to have aided preservice teachers in noticing their actual experience, and being with it, rather than trying to change it, even when it is uncomfortable.

Experiencing and embracing a full range of emotions, even ones that are challenging, aids our identities in becoming more multidimensional and is part of developing one's authenticity as a person and educator. Cultivating an open heart and developing emotional capacity in this way also increases educators' effectiveness with facilitating the social-emotional competence of their own students.

Theme Three: Relational Competence

Teaching is an inherently interactive profession. Educators need to be connected enough with the inner dimensions of their lives and selves that they can apply that wisdom to their interactions with others as they communicate intentionally with words and actions with students, colleagues, and families. Preservice teachers' written and oral comments suggest that the engaged teaching framework bolstered their relational skills. One's relational competence is a vital component of the inner core, including one's authenticity, which "extends beyond the individual" to be "other-directed as well" (Kreber et al., 2007; Weimer, 2011).

During an interview, one teacher candidate used a metaphor of hair braiding to describe her perception of the close interplay between teachers and students. She credited the five dimensions with helping her realize how much influence her P–12 students' identities, beliefs, and emotions have on her, and similarly, how much her own being and sense of self and personality influence her students.

Another teacher candidate described how the engaged teaching framework, especially the dimensions of being present, engaging the self-observer, and cultivating an open heart, helped her learn how to moderate her own emotional responses to students:

> One thing I will begin to practice now before I get into the classroom is the act of not *reacting* but *responding*. By being aware of the negative emotions rising, or anger wanting to take over, I can pause and allow it to fade until I can respectfully and mindfully go about conflict. It is important to be patient and conscious within the classroom because aggravating situations *will* arise.

This description represents a more compassionate, kind way of communicating that can be applied to interactions with anyone, not just one's students. Responding with patient self-awareness rather than automatic, knee-jerk reactions when triggered facilitates constructive relationships.

Other teacher candidates made specific reference to how the engaged teaching framework furthered their relational skills especially among their college peers. For example, one noted, "The process of being self-aware helped us be able to speak to our emotions and be more open to each other and more accepting in the process." Another commented, "The five dimensions have helped me to hold empathetic space for my peers so that we can have the opportunity to work through the challenging, conflicting content."

As another preservice teacher described, "[The five dimensions framework] allows me to really know what I'm feeling and to understand why. I have really learned to recognize what my triggers are and then being able to work through them." This passage illustrates nicely the connection between the authentic self-knowledge that comes from nurturing one's inner core and the ability to interact with others from a place of self-awareness. It also demonstrates how this framework supports educators in *being with* one's actual experience without necessarily trying to change it.

These communication and interpersonal skills are particularly significant when discussing and responding to potentially heated topics such as race, racism, and privilege, which are investigated in the equity course. Preservice teachers' comments suggest that the five dimensions helped them to notice through embodied physical and emotional reactions when they were getting triggered, and then to communicate with more empathy and understanding when discussing these sensitive issues.

Notably, the dimensions appear to support teacher candidates' ability to self-monitor and self-regulate their emotions and associated actions, especially in stressful situations. These relational skills are fundamental components of the inner core and are relevant every day inside and outside of classrooms.

Data analysis also suggests that the engaged teaching framework assisted preservice teachers' ability to consider multiple perspectives. Many participants, for example, described how the five dimensions helped them respond more calmly to peers during their online case study discussions on topics of race, racism, sexism, privilege, religious diversity, and other potentially heated issues. This quote is representative of many interview comments: "I remember feeling like I need to take a few deep breaths before I write this [online case study response]. . . . I engaged the five dimensions in that moment specifically so [my thoughts] wouldn't come out inflamed."

In the following interview passage, another teacher candidate went into more detail describing what happens inside of himself when he encounters views or opinions that are opposed to his and how he was able to apply the engaged teaching framework to hold that dissonance in a productive way:

> If people present a belief that is counter to what I believe and incorrect based on what we're thinking about, then I get angry, and I want to tell them what the real way, what the true way, is. I think it's those situations that are really challenging for me still.
>
> That's working with multiple dimensions in that when I engage the self-observer and sit presently with what I'm feeling, I find that I have a lot of sadness and anger about what I perceive to be the ignorance of humanity and our incapability to make change and to grow and to treat other people with respect. I kind of have a lot of anger about that. I'm working on cultivating the open heart there so that there can be more space for something more positive and more optimistic.

The passages above illustrate the potential of the five dimensions to support educators in developing a broader, more open and accepting stance toward views and opinions that differ from their own. These differences arise frequently in interactions among people from diverse racial, ethnic, socioeconomic, gender, and linguistic backgrounds (as is the case in our courses and in twenty-first-century society in general) and can become polarizing and distancing if the conversation participants have not had opportunities to pay attention to and develop the inner dimensions of their lives.

CONCLUSION

The Five Dimensions of Engaged Teaching framework provides a powerful resource for educators to cultivate their *inner core* within the context of the *common core* (Michalec, 2013), thereby fostering sustainability. Experiential practice with and critical reflection on the five dimensions using contemplative pedagogy appears to encourage educators to stay true to their authentic selves and respond with open-hearted compassion to the many challenging situations, emotional triggers, and diverse people and perspectives that contemporary educators face on a daily basis, both inside and outside of the high-pressure environment of contemporary schooling. The engaged teaching framework can influence not only how and why educators teach, but who they are as human beings.

ESSENTIAL IDEAS TO CONSIDER

Weaver and Wilding's (2013) framework in *The Five Dimensions of Engaged Teaching* can help educators at any level engage in contemplative introspection and cultivate their *inner core* by:

- developing various forms of social and emotional competence for interacting with colleagues, students, and families;
- developing authenticity as one blends professional and personal identities, inner and outer selves;
- developing relational skills, including self-awareness and self-regulation of emotions, that can result in more compassionate, constructive communication.

REFERENCES

Barbezat, D. P., & Bush, M. (2014). *Contemplative practices in higher education: Powerful methods to transform teaching and learning.* San Francisco: Jossey-Bass.

Creswell, J. (2013). *Qualitative inquiry & research design* (3rd ed.). Thousand Oaks, CA: Sage.

Erickson, F. (1986). Qualitative methods in research on teaching. In M. Wittrock (Ed.), *Handbook of research on teaching* (3rd ed.) (pp. 119–161). New York: MacMillan.

Greene, W., & Kim, Y. (2014). Starting with the soul: Teaching in the "taboo" dimensions of the classroom. Proceedings of the Tenth International Conference on Self-Study in Teacher Education Practices (pp. 103–105).

Killingsworth, M. A., & Gilbert, D. T. (2010, November 12). A wandering mind is an unhappy mind. *Science, 330*(6006), 932. doi: 10.1126/science/1192439.

Kreber, C., Klampfleitner, M., McCune, V., Bayne, S., & Knottenbelt, M. (2007). What do you mean by "authentic"? A comparative review of the literature on conceptions of authenticity in teaching. *Adult Education Quarterly, 58*(1), 22–44.

Michalec, P. (2013). Common core and inner core: Co-collaborators in teacher preparation. *Curriculum and Teaching Dialogue, 15*(1–2), 27–36.

Newby, P. (2014). *Research methods for education* (2nd ed.). New York: Routledge.

Palmer, P. (1997). The heart of a teacher: Identity and integrity in teaching. *Change, 29*(6), 15–21.

Palmer, P. (2007). *The courage to teach: Exploring the inner landscape of a teacher's life: 10th anniversary edition.* San Francisco: Jossey-Bass.

Saldaña, J. (2012). *The coding manual for qualitative researchers* (2nd ed.). Thousand Oaks, CA: Sage.

Weaver, L., & Wilding, M. (2013). *The five dimensions of engaged teaching: A practical guide for educators.* Bloomington, IN: Solution Tree Press.

Weimer, M. (2011, October 2). Authenticity in teaching. *The Teaching Professor.* Retrieved from www.montana.edu/facultyexcellent/documents/AuthenticityinTeaching_article.pdf.

Chapter Nine

"There Was This Moment When I Realized"

A Framework for Examining Mindful Moments in Teaching

Kira J. Baker-Doyle, Arcadia University School of Education, Glenside, Pennsylvania

The majority of teacher education research on mindfulness and contemplative practices today examines the outcomes of students or teachers engaged in formal mindfulness training programs (Gold et al., 2010; Meiklejohn et al., 2012; Roeser et al., 2012). However, an individual can be mindful without participating in a formal program or practice.

Mindfulness Theory (Langer, 1992) understands mindfulness to be a unique psychological state of being. Mindful moments are associated with a shift in previous thinking and a heightened awareness about one's contexts or experiences. During these moments individuals can feel vulnerable and afraid because their beliefs about the world and their identities are challenged. Yet they can also feel empowered by newfound possibilities for transformation.

This chapter provides a framework, informed by Langer's Mindfulness Theory, which can help teachers and teacher educators identify moments of "mindfulness." Furthermore, it describes contexts that nurture constructive emotions during moments of mindfulness based on the results of a study of the emotional ecologies of teachers' mindful moments.

THE MINDFULNESS THEORY FRAMEWORK FOR TEACHING

Mindfulness practice, which has roots in Buddhism, has emerged primarily as a method of stress reduction in Western medicine for persons suffering from chronic physical and mental illnesses (Asher, 2003; Kabat-Zinn & Hanh, 2009). Research on these practices shows that such practices not only reduce stress but they also improve cognition and physical health (Williams & Penman, 2012). Due to the positive effects, mindfulness has been a topic of interest to psychologists in recent years.

A leading scholar in the field of psychology of mindfulness is Ellen Langer. Langer developed Mindfulness Theory in 1992, a psychological theory that aims to characterize the difference between a mindful and mindless state of being. Langer's mindfulness concept stands in contrast to several other conceptual understandings of the term, including mindfulness as personality trait, a series of practices, or a spiritual concept. Instead, Langer defines mindfulness as a specific, psychological state of being.

The Mindfulness Theory psychological framework suggests that a person inhabits a state of mindfulness if he or she (1) creates new categories (schema) for understanding continuously (as opposed to being entrapped in rigid categories), (2) is open to new information or ways of thinking/doing, and (3) has an implicit awareness of more than one perspective, and more generally, (4) has an awareness of the larger context or environment (Langer, 1992, 1997; Langer & Moldoveanu, 2000).

The Mindfulness Theory Framework for Teaching (MTFT) (Table 9.1) is an analytic rubric based on Langer's definition and framework that was developed for the study presented in this chapter. In this research, the MTFT was used to identify and analyze teachers' mindful moments, which occurred primarily when they taught or reflected upon their work. The four axioms identified by Langer are the standards of the framework, and the descriptors provide examples of these axioms.

THE MTFT FRAMEWORK APPLIED: A STUDY OF TEACHERS' MINDFUL MOMENTS

The MTFT framework was used to analyze data from a two-year ethnographic research project of ten high school English teachers who were engaged in a collaborative inquiry group (the Cavanaugh-Astor Teacher Collaborative, or CATC).

The group primarily worked together to develop curriculum, and the study took place in a U.S. high school that was characterized by a focus on teacher accountability based on student test scores and a culture of uniformity. The research questions guiding the study were: What do mindful mo-

Table 9.1. Mindfulness Theory Framework for Teaching (MTFT). Mindful moments were characterized as events or brief periods of time in teachers' lives in which their thinking or actions reflected the axioms listed in the top row. The descriptors are examples of characteristics that reflected the axioms.

Continuous creation of new categories	Openness to new information	Implicit awareness of more than one perspective	Conscious attention to larger context
• Developing/ noticing new explanations or perspectives on practices, beliefs, or phenomena.	• Exploring and seeking alternatives to their own ways of thinking/ doing.	• Thinking about one's thinking in relation to one's own past or others' ideas.	• Historical perspective of change.
• Belief in the possibility of change in one's own beliefs/ practices.	• Active listening.	• Identifying other possibilities.	• Awareness of complex relationships/ communication patterns.
• Shifts in pedagogy	• Willingness to listen to others' perspectives.	• Non-absolutism.	
• Awareness of inner voice(s)— the stories we tell ourselves.	• Questioning.		

ments look like for CATC teachers? And, what emotions are prevalent for teachers during moments of mindfulness?

In addition to the MTFT, Zembylas's (2005, 2007) "emotional ecologies" model was used to analyze teachers' emotions. This model provides a means to describe how emotions develop and change in complex systems of relationships. A core concept in this model is the "emotive" (Reddy, 1997), which is a performance of an emotion that brings about a response or change in social context. This concept is used to identify the ways in which emotions operate in three social realms: the individual (self), relational (interpersonal), and sociopolitical (within the larger community).

Another important concept in Zembylas's model is the notion of the "emotional regime," which is a school's normative expectations about what teachers should feel and do. This concept places a spotlight on the normative "moral purposes" in a school community, and can serve to reveal potential conflicts between teachers' own purposes and those of the school administration or broader school community.

Zembylas and others (Hargreaves, 1998; Nias, 1993) suggest that when teachers' moral purposes are opposed to a schools' emotional regime, teachers can become "demoralized." This study illustrates how mindful moments of collaboration and creative production foster resistance to demoralization and a sense of emotional freedom in teaching.

Findings: The Emotional Ranges and Contexts of Teachers' Mindful Moments

The data were analyzed with the use of a qualitative analysis software tool (Dedoose, 2016), which allowed the location and organization of the data around themes.Ten personal events in participants' experiences and reflections were identified that met the criteria of a mindful moment under the Mindfulness Theory Framework for Teaching. The emotives that teachers expressed during these mindful moments were examined across the realms of the individual, relational, and sociopolitical (see Table 9.2 for summary). Through this process, several themes emerged in the data.

Mindful Moments, Negative Emotives, and Isolation

First, not all moments of mindfulness elicited positive emotions; in several cases, teachers' mindful moments came with feelings of demoralization and deep sorrow. Yet, these negative mindful moments all had a single commonality: they all occurred when teachers were isolated, and not connected or collaborating with others.

A good example of this phenomena is illustrated in Bobbi's story. Bobbi was a teacher in the English department with more than fifteen years of teaching experience. During interviews, she described a moment in her teaching in which she began to question her purpose and approaches. This realization came after rising frustration in seeing that her students were not reading or engaging in the books that she had assigned. Despite her frustration, her approach to teaching was generally the accepted practice in the school at that time. Below, she describes the moment:

> About five years ago, standing in front of the classroom, talking about a book we read, and I was like, "This is ridiculous. Why am I giving them a test on this . . . I just felt like it was just futile. I felt like they're not reading, even though I'm excited about it. There's so much that's not going on and I just felt like . . . I felt like I was doing all this work and I was doing all this. . . . I had all this passion and I was the one pushing all of it and it just wasn't working anymore. I think it used to work. (Bobbi, Interview, 2013)

This change in consciousness occurred during a time when Bobbi was not collaborating frequently with colleagues. Eventually, Bobbi's awareness al-

Table 9.2. Emotives of teachers during moments of mindfulness. Mindful moments are characterized as isolated (occurred when teacher was working by themselves), collaborative (occurred when teacher was collaborating with others), and creative/productive (occurred when teacher was producing a creative work).

Moment Title	Characteristic of Context	Individual Emotives	Relational Emotives	Sociopolitical Emotives
Bobbi #1	Isolated	Futility, sadness	Awareness of student disinterest	Frustration in projecting school emotional regime
Cory #1	Isolated	Sadness, death of spirit	Frustration	Not fitting in; no space in school emotional regime
Howard #1	Isolated	Bored, tired, purposeless	Awareness of student disinterest	Boredom in projecting school emotional regime
Liz	Collaborative	Hope, happiness	Compassion, openness with colleagues	Excitement in changing school emotional regime
Bobbi #2	Collaborative	Freedom, possibility	Freedom—letting go of control	Freedom from emotional regime
Cory #2	Collaborative	Happy, satisfied	Open, vulnerable	Feeling accepted/ noticed
Howard #2	Collaborative	Hopeful, purposeful	Openness/ wonder—there's value in others	Freedom; motivation to change school
Rebecca	Creative/ Productive	Satisfied	Curious	Feeling accepted/ noticed
Julie	Creative/ Productive	Excitement, happiness, joy in work	Compassion (bonding, understanding, vulnerability with students)	Excitement in seeing changing school emotional regime
Dory	Creative/ Productive	Happiness, fulfillment, excitement	Wondering, curious, vulnerable, open	Space outside of emotional regime/ emotional freedom

lowed her to be open to new approaches, and when offered the opportunity to participate in the CATC group and rewrite her curriculum, she became fully engaged in the process.

This moment met the criteria for being a mindful moment in all four categories of the rubric. Bobbi noticed new explanations and perspectives about her practice, she questioned her practice and became open to new ideas, she reflected on her own thinking, and she had an historical comparison to her thinking before and after. In looking at her individual emotives, she shared a sense of futility and frustration. Looking relationally, she was aware of student disengagement. Finally, from a sociopolitical standpoint, Bobbi's mindful moment triggered anxiety around projecting the school's emotional regime, which supported the traditional approaches that she employed.

Positive Emotives, Collaboration, and Creative Production During Mindful Moments

Positive emotions occurred generally during moments when teachers either had experiences collaborating with others or constructing/producing creative work. These two themes were evident in emotives across all social realms. Individual-level emotives ranged between happiness and despair. During isolated moments of mindfulness, teachers' individual-level emotives were despair and boredom. Yet in collaborative and production-centered mindful moments, teachers' individual emotives were typically happiness and satisfaction.

Cory's experience working with CATC illustrates this finding on individual-level emotives. Cory became involved in CATC and embraced the group as a source of inspiration and support. One day, she was teaching a lesson on writing open letters, and she decided to write her own letter as well. This decision propelled her into another moment of mindfulness, in which she reflected back on her "Sad Teacher Self," a self-proclaimed emotive, and spoke to it with compassion and hope. Below is an excerpt from her letter:

> No one's even pretending this is working, least of all you. But trust me, things can change. Will you suspend your disbelief long enough to re-discover your possibility?
>
> This is how it will work: you'll give yourself permission to try things, new things, crazy things, out-of-the-box, stand-on-your-head, wiggle your toes in the wind kinds of things. You'll go where the energy is and stop doing stuff just because some ancient crumbling teacher manual of yore says it works.
>
> You'll get vulnerable and you'll get brave and you'll start writing with your kids. You'll remember that teaching and learning are symbiotic and if you want to be an inspiring teacher, you must be an inspired learner. Take risks, receive feedback, try a difficult task again—and then again. (Cory, Open Letter, 2012)

Cory's openness to possibility and change, hope, sense of multiple stories and voices, and commitment to active listening are all hallmarks of a mindful moment.

This way of thinking represented a major shift for Cory, who, like Bobbi, was fearful of letting go of control, yet that fear seemed to control her as well. Cory's individual emotives changed significantly over her time in working with CATC. Furthermore, she developed more trusting relationships with students and her colleagues. In addition to her self-report of increased trust, three other participants concurred with her statement and noted that they collaborated with her more frequently than they had previously. From a sociopolitical perspective, Cory felt safe challenging traditional school norms.

In the relational realm (interpersonal relationships), emotives ranged from compassion/interest to frustration. On the positive end, teachers generally spoke of the hope and wonder that others' ideas brought them, all of which occurred through collaboration and creative endeavors. Negative relational emotives included frustration and confusion; teachers were aware that they were having trouble understanding students. These negative mindful moments occurred before the teachers had strong collaborative relationships with others in their department.

Howard's stories of mindfulness before and after his involvement with CATC provide a good example of these differences. As with Bobbi and Cory, Howard was a seasoned teacher who developed second thoughts about continuing in the profession. Also similarly, he rarely collaborated with others at the time. While he felt that he had found a method that "worked," he was bored with the routine. He also had a sense that students could be more engaged than they were in the activities he had been doing. He reflected on a moment of awareness that occurred for him at that time:

> I think there was a point, maybe three years ago . . . the thought occurred to me that I can't possibly keep doing what I was doing for twenty more years. It didn't matter if I changed curriculum or year, how I was doing what I was doing was not going to sustain me for another twenty years. (Howard, Interview, 2013)

The moment of awareness is considered a mindful moment because he began to think about the possibility of change, questioned his role, considered other options, and took a historical perspective on his experience. He felt bored and purposeless, and, relationally, also sensed that his students felt the same. He did not exhibit a sense of threat from the emotional regime of the school, but did seem disinterested and disconnected with it.

Howard experienced a radical shift in his pedagogical approach after joining CATC. Whereas before he was simply aware that things could not go on the way they were going, in his second mindful moment, he made a conscious decision to invite change. His second mindful moment might be better described as a series of moments or decisions. For Howard, each time he committed himself to attending a CATC meeting, he was reminding himself that it was time to change. In a reflective essay, he wrote, "Participating in CATC every week is my pledge to myself to just evolve in a way that makes me ultimately happy and proud and satisfied."

Howard's choice to commit to the group was a choice to be mindful, and was, in itself, a moment of mindfulness. When asked to explain why CATC was important to him, he talked about the valuable relationships that he developed through the group, several of which he did not think would have developed if not for the group.

Lastly, analysis of teachers' emotives in the sociopolitical realm (school-wide micro-politics) revealed that collaborative or production-related moments of mindfulness helped teachers create spaces of emotional freedom from the schools "emotional regime" (or the accepted norms of emotions for the school culture), and in several cases, they challenged the emotional regime to become more accepting of risk taking, vulnerability, and compassion for students and colleagues.

For isolated moments of mindfulness, teachers were more aware of the emotional regime, and were thus frustrated at the thought of trying to fit the mold. The school's norms were centered on preparation for high-stakes standardization, emphasizing competitive, outcomes-based pedagogical practices.

Rebecca's efforts to bring a creative, production-based orientation into her classroom through writing illustrates how her engagement in creative processes fostered mindful moments of awareness, eliciting a sense agency and freedom in her work. Rebecca was a veteran teacher who also had several previous careers in the creative arts before entering the teaching profession.

A writer, artist, and actor, Rebecca sought opportunities to be creative in every career she held. As an English teacher, she hoped to inspire a love of creativity in her students as well. Yet, at the time of this study, she had been strongly contemplating retirement; she was not feeling inspired, nor did she sense curiosity in her students. Over her summers, she had been taking graduate writing classes and thought perhaps she would leave teaching to write a book.

Then, she reported, one day her thinking shifted. She had a guest in her classroom, a member of CATC and a professor at a local university. He did a demonstration lesson and he wrote *with* the students. CATC strongly supported the idea of teachers being writers with their students. In this moment, she realized that she could merge her interests. She could write and teach at the same time. It was a mindful moment, one in which Rebecca realized that there were more possibilities and ways of thinking and doing.

Prior to this moment of realization, Rebecca had felt that she was not allowed to engage in this practice under the school regime. She had felt isolated and shunned when she experimented with more creative attempts at teaching. Her response had been to retreat into privacy. Here she described the change from isolation to freedom:

> I've got to do a lot of the things I wanted to do. I don't need to be anybody [in authority], so I had to retreat as a result . . . in [that] moment, I'm all done . . . I'm done and you won't know me and I won't know you. It's not necessarily a great way to be but it's just . . . I'm just sharing. And that's what it had become and I couldn't be luckier . . . that I have been given freedom to [shape] the whole creative writing piece of things. (Rebecca, Interview, 2013)

As such, Rebecca experienced a personal sense of freedom and a relational sense of greater curiosity and openness in connecting with others. She was less afraid of the sociopolitical regime. She felt more accepted and noticed by the school.

Dory decided to engage in creative writing alongside her students, which elicited a similar kind of mindful moment to that experienced by Rebecca. In an essay reflecting on this moment, she wrote:

> After a year of writing with my students in a transformative writing project and an attempt at shifting traditional educational paradigms, I think I've, unbeknownst to myself, re-found myself and my own voice as a writer that thinks in writerly ways, influencing my own life through the writing work. I couldn't encourage my students to write for a real audience, not just the teacher, without doing it myself. This is the impact of transformative LIFE WORK. Teaching is not just about what happens during the school day, but about what happens after to impact our lives and our surrounding communities; that includes myself, not just my students. (Dory, Written Reflection)

Dory's reflection tells of a moment in which she demonstrates a sense of inner awareness, transformation, connection with others, and openness to multiple perspectives. Her ongoing work as a writer in collaboration with her students provided a context in which she was able to process and reflect upon her own experiences and those of others. As with Rebecca, writing set the stage for a moment that elicited a sense of hope, possibility, and satisfaction. Relationally, Dory's openness to vulnerability strengthened her compassion and empathy for her students. She also created her own space, beyond the emotional regime of the school, for her beliefs and practices.

CONCLUSION

Teachers experience moments of mindfulness throughout their careers in which they develop a greater awareness of their beliefs, pedagogy, and relationships with others. The MTFT framework provides a useful tool for identifying and analyzing mindful moments in teaching. This chapter provided an example of the application of this framework to analyze the mindful moments and socioemotional states of a small group of teachers. The outcomes of the analysis here reveal how moments of mindfulness can reveal one's suffering, triggering deep personal changes, and can also strengthen teachers' abilities to forge paths for resistance to demoralization.

Furthermore, the findings support previous research that demonstrates the value of collaborative work in fostering teaching well-being (Le Cornu, 2013; Puchner & Taylor, 2006; Zembylas & Barker, 2007) and hooks' (1994) and Hanh's (2013) arguments that one should be "engaged" in mindful acts (beyond internal awareness/reflection). Thus, in addition to offering a useful framework for scholars, teacher educators, and teachers to identify moments of mindfulness and two strategies, the analysis here provides suggestions for ways to foster positive and empowering moments of mindfulness.

ESSENTIAL IDEAS TO CONSIDER

- A mindful moment in teaching is defined as a time when a teacher experiences a shift in previous thinking and a heightened awareness about their teaching context or experience.
- Some mindful moments can result in negative feelings about teaching. These primarily occur during times of isolation.
- Mindful moments that result in positive feelings about teaching occur during times in which teachers collaborate and reflect with others, and when teachers use creative practices such as writing to express themselves.

REFERENCES

Asher, N. (2003). Engaging difference: Towards a pedagogy of interbeing. *Teaching Education, 14*(3), 235–247.
Baker-Doyle, K. J., & Gustavson, L. (2015). Permission-seeking as an agentive tool for transgressive teaching: An ethnographic study of teachers organizing for curricular change. *Journal of Educational Change, 17*(1), 51–84.
Dedoose. (2016). *Dedoose: Great research made easy.* Retrieved September 14, from http://www.dedoose.com/.
Gold, E., Smith, A., Hopper, I., Herne, D., Tansey, G., & Hulland, C. (2010). Mindfulness-based stress reduction (MBSR) for primary school teachers. *Journal of Child and Family Studies, 19*(2), 184–189.
Hanh, T. N. (2013). *Work: How to find joy and meaning in each hour of the day.* Berkeley, CA: Parallax Press.
Hargreaves, A. (1998). The emotional practice of teaching. *Teaching and Teacher Education, 14*(8), 835–854.
hooks, b. (1994). *Teaching to transgress: Education as the practice of freedom.* New York: Routledge.

Kabat-Zinn, J., & Hanh, T. N. (2009). *Full catastrophe living: Using the wisdom of your body and mind to face stress, pain, and illness*. New York: Random House.

Langer, E. J. (1992). Matters of mind: Mindfulness/mindlessness in perspective. *Consciousness and Cognition, 1*(3), 289–305.

Langer, E. J. (1997). *The power of mindful learning* (Vol. xii). Cambridge, MA: Da Capo Press.

Langer, E. J., & Moldoveanu, M. (2000). Mindfulness research and the future. *Journal of Social Issues, 56*(1), 129–139.

Le Cornu, R. (2013). Building early career teacher resilience: The role of relationships. *Australian Journal of Teacher Education, 38*(4).

Meiklejohn, J., Phillips, C., Freedman, M. L., Griffin, M. L., Biegel, G., Roach, A., Saltzman, A. (2012). Integrating mindfulness training into K–12 education: Fostering the resilience of teachers and students. *Mindfulness, 3*(4), 291–307.

Nias, J. (1993). Changing times, changing identities: Grieving for a lost self. In R. G. Burgess (Ed.), *Educational research and evaluation: For policy and practice* (pp. 139–156). London: Falmer Press.

Puchner, L. D., & Taylor, A. R. (2006). Lesson study, collaboration and teacher efficacy: Stories from two school-based math lesson study groups. *Teaching and Teacher Education, 22*(7), 922–934.

Reddy, W. M. (1997). Against constructionism: The historical ethnography of emotions. *Current Anthropology, 38*(3), 327–351.

Roeser, R. W., Skinner, E., Beers, J., & Jennings, P. A. (2012). Mindfulness training and teachers' professional development: An emerging area of research and practice. *Child Development Perspectives, 6*(2), 167–173.

Williams, M., & Penman, D. (2012). *Mindfulness: An eight-week plan for finding peace in a frantic world*. New York: Rodale.

Zembylas, M. (2005). Beyond teacher cognition and teacher beliefs: The value of the ethnography of emotions in teaching. *International Journal of Qualitative Studies in Education, 18*(4), 465–487.

Zembylas, M. (2007). Emotional ecology: The intersection of emotional knowledge and pedagogical content knowledge in teaching. *Teaching and Teacher Education, 23*(4), 355–367.

Zembylas, M., & Barker, H. B. (2007). Teachers' spaces for coping with change in the context of a reform effort. *Journal of Educational Change, 8*(3), 235–256.

Index

About the Editors and Contributors

Elizabeth Hope Dorman, PhD, is associate professor of teacher education at Fort Lewis College, in Durango, Colorado, where she teaches graduate and undergraduate students in secondary, K–12, teacher leadership, and elementary education programs. Her research interests include the integration and effects of mindfulness and contemplative practices and pedagogies on teacher development of social-emotional competence, particularly in diverse contexts and courses that address multicultural perspectives and equity issues.

Kathryn Byrnes, PhD, is the Baldwin program director in the Center for Learning and Teaching at Bowdoin College, and faculty member at the Teachings in Mindful Education (TiME) Institute in Maine. She served as board president of the Mindfulness in Education Network (MiEN), and taught in-person and online courses on Mindful Education at Lesley University and Bowdoin College. Her scholarship and professional development work focuses on the integration of contemplative pedagogy in educational contexts.

Jane E. Dalton, PhD, is assistant professor of art education at the University of North Carolina at Charlotte teaching art education and studio art. Her research interests include arts-based learning, transformative learning, and contemplative practices to promote embodied learning. A textile artist, Jane's work has been exhibited throughout the United States. She is the coauthor of *The Compassionate Classroom: Lessons that Nurture Empathy and Wisdom* and author of the blog *The Expressive Teacher* (http://theexpressiveteacher.com).

***

123

Kira J. Baker-Doyle is an assistant professor of education at Arcadia University. She is the author of *The Networked Teacher: How New Teachers Build Social Networks for Professional Support* (2011) and a forthcoming book with Harvard Education Press about transformative teaching in a connected world.

Gayle L. Butaud holds an EdD in literacy from Sam Houston State University at Huntsville, Texas. She is currently a faculty member of the Department of Teacher Education and the director of Field Experience at Lamar University. Her research interests include preservice teachers, mentoring preservice teachers, literacy, and high-quality literacy instruction.

Jennifer Cannon is a PhD candidate in the Department of Teacher Education and Curriculum Studies at the University of Massachusetts, Amherst, and is a UCLA-certified mindfulness facilitator. Her areas of scholarship include critical theory, women of color feminism, decolonial theory, and contemplative pedagogy. Jennifer has been teaching in the field of social justice education for more than twenty-five years and serves as a diversity consultant and antiracist educator.

Lisa Flook is a scientist at the Center for Healthy Minds at the University of Wisconsin–Madison. She is involved in projects with preschool and elementary school students and teachers, parents, and preservice teachers to explore effective and sustainable ways of introducing mindfulness-based practices in school and community settings and assessing their effects through research.

M. Elizabeth Graue is the Sorenson Professor of Childhood Studies and the chair of the Department of Curriculum and Instruction at the University of Wisconsin–Madison.

William L. Greene is an educational psychologist and professor in the School of Education at Southern Oregon University. His scholarship focuses on transformative learning, social-emotional development, presence, and core reflection in the context of holistic teaching and learning practices. He cofounded the Teacher Education for the Future Project, an international collaboration of Pacific Circle Consortium member nations, and has served as coeditor of the *Pacific-Asian Education Journal*.

Matthew J. Hirshberg is a graduate student in the Center for Healthy Minds and the Department of Educational Psychology, both at the University of Wisconsin–Madison. A former teacher, Matt's research examines the possible benefits, for students and teachers, of integrating contemplative practice into educational contexts.

Younghee M. Kim is a child development specialist and professor in the School of Education at Southern Oregon University. Her scholarship includes holistic teaching and learning, core reflection approach to whole teacher development, human potential, presence, and contemplative education. She has served as coeditor of the *Pacific-Asian Education Journal* and is a coauthor of the book *Teaching and Learning from Within: A Core Reflection Approach to Quality and Inspiration in Education* (2013).

Per F. Laursen, PhD, is a professor at the Danish School of Education, Aarhus University, Copenhagen, Denmark. His research interests are in the fields of teacher education, curriculum theory, and teacher development. He is a teacher and supervisor at the MA in Education and at the MA in Educational Psychology among others, and supervisor of PhD students.

Roshmi Mishra is a secondary science public school teacher in New York State, an adjunct professor for the School of Education, Department of Curriculum and Instructions at the State University of New York at Oswego, and a certified yoga and meditation teacher. She is an ABD PhD student at Union Institute & University with a concentration in public policy and social change.

Evan E. Moss is a graduate student in the Department of Curriculum and Instruction at the University of Wisconsin–Madison. As a preservice teacher supervisor and a former middle school teacher, Evan is interested in how contemplative practice can help to innovate teacher education.

Shelley Murphy, PhD, is a lecturer in the Department of Curriculum, Teaching and Learning at the Ontario Institute for Studies in Education at the University of Toronto. She is also a researcher, author, speaker, education consultant, and former elementary teacher.

Anne Maj Nielsen, PhD, is an associate professor at the Danish School of Education, Aarhus University, Copenhagen, Denmark. Her research interests are in the fields of contemplative education and teaching, mindful awareness in teaching and teacher education, and aesthetic experience-based learning. Her research and teaching is inspired by phenomenology and cultural psychology. She is a teacher and supervisor at the MA in Educational Psychology, supervisor for PhD students, and is presently head of the Department of Educational Psychology, Aarhus University.

Elsie L. Olan is an assistant professor in the School of Teaching, Learning, and Leadership at the University of Central Florida. Her research interests and foci are in two areas, both which have grown from her professional work: (a) the role of language and writing, literacy, literature, and diversity in learning and teaching in language arts education and ST(R)E(A)M fields, and (b) in teaching and teacher education: teacher narratives, inquiry, and reflective practices in (national and international) teaching environments and professional development settings.

Vanessa M. Villate holds a PhD in curriculum and instruction from the University of Texas at Austin. She is currently an associate professor in teacher education at Lamar University. Her research interests include mindfulness in education and innovative teaching and learning environments.